Introduction to Java Spring Boot: Learning By Coding

by

AJ Henley Jr

Dave Wolf

Afua Ankomah

Jennifer Lee &

Victor Phimphachanh

A paperback edition of this was published in 2019 by AJ Henley.

The Introduction to Java Spring Boot copyright © 2019 by AJ Henley. All rights reserved. Printed in the United States of America. No part of this book may be used or reproduced in any manner whatsoever without written permission.

Learning By Coding books may be purchased for educational, business or sales promotional use. For information, please email ajhenley@gmail.com.

First Edition published 2019.

ISBN: 978-1088797242

CONTENTS

1.0	**GETTING STARTED**	**5**
1.00	Setting Up Your Environment	6
1.01	Hello World	9
1.02	Hello World with Variables	13
1.03	Hello World with External Variables	16
2.0	**ESSENTIAL TOOLS**	**19**
2.01	Handling Form Values - The Hard Way	20
2.02	Creating a Java Bean	23
2.03	Handling Form Values - The Easy Way	25
2.04	Form Validation	29
3.0	**DATA TOOLS**	**35**
3.01	Saving Data to a Database	36
3.02	Looping Through a List with Thymeleaf	40
3.03	Data Lifecycle Create/Retrieve/Update/Delete	47
3.04	Automatically Adding Records to the Database	55
3.05	Database Relationships - Many to Many	58
3.06	Database Relationships - One to Many	63
3.07	Database Relationships - One to One	69
4.0	**SECURITY**	**75**
4.01	Basic Security	76
4.02	Adding a Custom Login Page	80
4.03	Using Roles for Page Permissions	84
4.04	Using Database-based Authentication	88
4.05	Persisting Current User Information	96
4.06	Implementing User Registration	98
5.0	**DESIGN TOOLS**	**103**
5.01	Using Page Fragments with Thymeleaf	104
5.02	Adding Twitter Bootstrap using CDNs	108
5.03	Uploading images with Cloudinary	110
5.04	Adding Twitter Bootstrap directly to Spring Boot	118
5.05	Custom Error Pages	122
6.0	**DEPLOYMENT TOOLS**	**125**
6.01	Deploying to Heroku	126
6.02	Deploying to AWS	128

HOW TO READ THIS BOOK

Preface

This book is a beginner's guide to Spring Boot 2.0. The purpose of this book is to give users step by step instructions on how to implement fundamental web development techniques in Spring Boot 2.0.

This book covers several topics individually so that it is much easier to grasp and use in real-life projects.

Who this book for

This book is for anyone interested in developing applications using the Spring Framework, and specifically, Spring Boot 2. The readers may have prior experience of Spring Boot, but it isn't required, as even beginners can benefit from the content of this book.

This book expects the readers to have some level of understanding of programming with Java.

What this book covers

Section 1, Getting Started

Helps you setup your development environment so you can write your first Spring Boot programs. Topics covered include the basics of routing, templates and using dependencies.

Section 2, Essential Tools

Takes you from handling form data manually and quickly advances to more advanced techniques for passing and validating data using Java Beans.

Section 3, Data Tools

Introduces the JPA persistence library for using a database with your Spring Boot application. You'll learn how to save, update, retrieve and delete data without writing actual SQL. You'll also learn about the different relationships that exist between tables.

HOW TO READ THIS BOOK (CONT)

Section 4, Security

Presents a great introduction to securing your application using Spring Security. After implementing basic security in a Spring Boot application you'll customize the login page, add user registration and control page permissions with roles.

Section 5, Design Tools

Shows how to implement the Bootstrap framework, organize site assets, create custom error pages, and incorporate a content distribution network (CDN) for handling images.

Section 6, Deployment Tools

Round out your skill set with examples that illustrate how to deploy your site on the internet using Heroku or Amazon Web Services (AWS).

To get the most out of this book

You need knowledge of the following:
- Basic Java (you should be able to create a console application)
- HTML and CSS
- Database Design and basic SQL

The code bundle for the book is also hosted on Git Hub at https://github.com/lbcbooks/IntroductionToJavaSpringBoot. The Git Hub repository will always contain the latest version of the code.

How to Read this Book

Each lesson starts with a step by step walk through using IntelliJ. Following the instructions, the What's Going On section includes an in-depth discussion of the steps you just followed. Also on the page is a list of the correct library imports listed under the keywords or commands that need them. Finally, at the end of each lesson are questions to help cement your understanding of the material and, usually, a coding exercise to test your complete comprehension.

GETTING STARTED

1.00 Setting Up Your Environment
1.01 Hello World
1.02 Hello World with Variables
1.03 Hello World with External Variables

1.00 SETTING UP YOUR ENVIRONMENT

OBJECTIVES

- Installing Git
- Installing the Heroku CLI
- Installing the Java Development Kit (JDK)
- Installing Intellij

THE WALKTHROUGH

1. Installing Git
   - Open https://git-scm.com in your browser
   - Download the installer for your machine
   - Run the installer application (accept the defaults for any questions)

2. Installing the Heroku CLI
   - Open https://devcenter.heroku.com/articles/heroku-cli in your browser
   - Download the installer for your machine
   - Run the installer application (accept the defaults for any questions)

3. Installing the JDK
   - Open http://www.oracle.com/technetwork/java/javase/downloads/index.html in your browser
   - Click on the JDK download button
   - Download the JDK installer for your machine
   - Run the installer application (accept the defaults for any questions)

4. Installing IntelliJ IDEA
   - Open https://www.jetbrains.com/idea/ in your browser
   - Download the installer for your machine
   - If you are a student in a college or university, go to https://www.jetbrains.com/student/ and using your campus email, register to get a one year free license
   - Run the installer application (accept the defaults for any questions)

5. Reboot your machine

1.00 SETTING UP YOUR ENVIRONMENT

6. Editing Default File Templates
   - Run IntelliJ IDEA
   - With IntelliJ IDEA running and no project open, you should see the Welcome screen.
   - Select the Configure drop-down in the lower right corner
   - Select the item at the top of the drop-down (it's probably Settings or Preferences)
   - Select Editor on the left hand side of the screen and then click File and Code Templates on the right
   - With HTML File selected in the middle, edit the template to the right to look like this:

```html
<!DOCTYPE html>
<html lang="en" xmlns:th="www.thymeleaf.org">
  <head>
    <meta charset="UTF-8" />
    <title>#[[$Title$]]#</title>
  </head>
  <body>
    #[[$END$]]#
  </body>
</html>
```

   - Click OK

WHAT'S GOING ON

The software you are downloading are the tools you will need to write, compile and deploy java applications from your own machine.

WRITING YOUR CODE

The software that is used to write Java programs and especially Spring Boot programs is an IDE or Integrated Development Environment. The leading IDE for Java is Eclipse (which is available at www.eclipse.org). But the best IDE for Java, in my opinion, is IntelliJ IDEA (which is available at www.jetbrains.com/idea). If you are a student, you can get IntelliJ IDEA for a year for free, but if not, you can work through the exercises in this book by using the 14-day demo version.

COMPILING YOUR CODE

In order to compile Java programs on your machine, you will need to download the JDK or Java Development Kit. This software is available on the Oracle website at www.oracle.com. You will need to install the proper JDK for your machine and reboot it before you will be able to get any of the lessons to work.

DEPLOYING YOUR CODE

To save your code and move completed programs to our hosting company, Heroku.com, you need to install the Heroku CLI and git. These will make it possible submit your code to source control and to transmit that code to Heroku.

CUSTOMIZING THE HTML TEMPLATE

To ease your use of HTML templates and reduce the possibility of error, we customize our HTML template to include the attribute **xmlns:th="www.thymeleaf.org"** to our html tag. This makes it easier to work with Thymeleaf, our template engine, and now you will not run the chance of forgetting it.

1.01 HELLO WORLD WITH A TEMPLATE

LEARNING OBJECTIVES
- Creating a Spring Boot Application
- Creating a Controller
- Creating a Thymeleaf Template

THE WALKTHROUGH

1. **Create a Spring Boot Application**
   - Go to the menu and click File -> New Project
   - On the left-hand side click on Spring Initializr and click Next on the lower right
   - Go to the Name field and set the name to SpringBoot_101 and click Next on the lower right
   - Select the dependencies for web and thymeleaf
     - On the left column click on Web and then click the checkbox next to Spring Web Starter in the middle column
     - On the left column click on Template Engines and then click the checkbox next to Thymeleaf in the middle column
     - Click the Next button in the lower right hand corner
   - Change the project name field to **SpringBoot_101** and click Finish
   - The wizard may take some time to finish, but if you are asked if you want to Add as Maven Project then click the provided link
   - You know it is finished when there is a leaf with a power button in the upper right hand corner of your screen like in *Screen 1.01.1*.

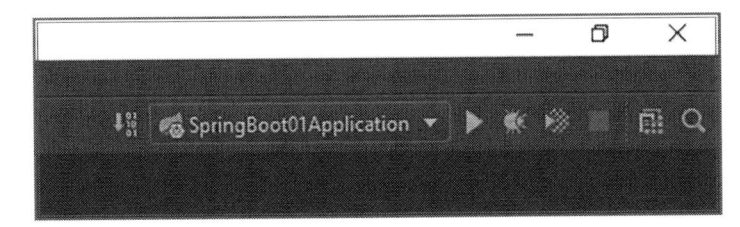

Screen 1.01.1

Screen 1.01.2

2. **Create a Controller**
   - Click on the triangle next to your application's folder in the left hand menu, this expands that folder
   - Expand the src folder -> Expand the main folder -> Expand the java folder
   - You should now be seeing something like *Screen 1.01.2*.
   - Right click on com.example.demo and click New -> Class
   - Name it HomeController.java

1.01 HELLO WORLD WITH A TEMPLATE

- Edit it to look like this:

```
@Controller
public class HomeController {
    @RequestMapping("/")
    public String homePage(){
        return "index";
    }
}
```

3. **Create a Template**
   - Expand the resources folder inside of the main folder
   - Right click on templates and click New -> Html
   - Name it index.html
   - Edit the empty body tag (<body></body>) to look like this:

   ```
   <body>
       <h2>Hello World!</h2>
   </body>
   ```

4. **Run your application**
   - To run the application click the run button in the upper right hand corner like in *Screen 1.01.3*.

5. **View your Application**
   - Open Google Chrome and type in the URL http://localhost:8080 and hit enter. You should Hello World! displayed as it is in *Screen 1.01.4*.

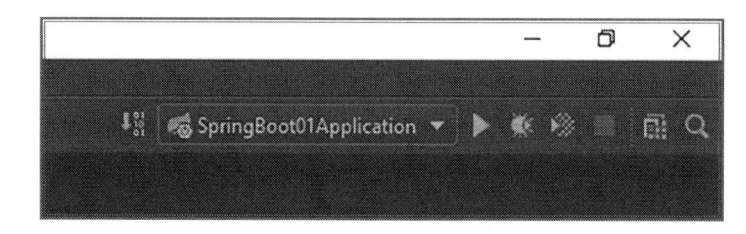

Screen 1.01.3

Screen 1.01.4

IMPORTS

CONTROLLER
org.springframework.stereotype.Controller

REQUESTMAPPING
org.springframework.web.bind.annotation.RequestMapping

1.01 HELLO WORLD WITH A TEMPLATE

WHAT'S GOING ON

Lines 1 and 2 of HomeController.java import the classes into your project that make the **@Controller** and **@RequestMapping** annotations work.

The **@Controller** annotation tells the compiler that there is a list of paths in this file that the user can browse to within the HomeController class. By using this annotation, we have made the HomeController like a phone directory or reference list for our application, where all the routes are mapped out.

@RequestMapping indicates what path or end point the user will visit. The method following the **@RequestMapping** annotation is run each time that the path is used. In this case, the default path is the only path that is specified out.

When a user browses to http://localhost:8080 (or the default path on the port that has been set for the application if 8080 is not in use), then the application will return a template (html file) called index.html from the templates folder. The extension is left out because the application assumes the extension, and appends it to the filename at runtime.

WHAT'S A PATH?

A path is a set of directions from the base URL that your application can respond to. If your site is served up at http://localhost:8080, then telling a user to go to http://localhost:8080/add means that the path is "/add".

Telling a user to load http://localhost:8080/ means that the path is "/".

The default path is indicated by using ("/"). This means that when you visit http://localhost:8080 or http://localhost:8080/ when the application is running, the application will run the code in the method following the **@RequestMapping** annotation for the default path.

@RequestMapping maps out both GET and POST requests.

The easiest way to think about GET and POST requests is that you use GET requests in your application when the user is getting information from the server. It results in a response that the user can see - e.g. browsing to a page. A user can type parameters in the URL to provide additional information, e.g. his/her name, and those will provide extra information to the application that it can use to show the user more information based on those parameters. Since the parameters in the URL are visible to the user, make sure that you use GET requests for parameters that are not sensitive (e.g. NO PASSWORDS!!)

You will use POST requests for all routes that are posting or sending information to the server. If a user enters details in a form, use a POST request so that when the user clicks the "Submit" button, the details will be sent to the server and will be hidden from view (i.e. they will not be in the URL).

1.01 HELLO WORLD WITH A TEMPLATE

For more about GET and POST requests, see these articles:

http://www.diffen.com/difference/GET-vs-POST-HTTP-Requests
https://www.w3schools.com/tags/ref_httpmethods.asp

By default, **@RequestMapping** maps to a GET request.

WHAT'S A TEMPLATE?

A template is a blueprint for a dynamic page. A template is different from a static page because what you will see can change depending on the user who is logged in, and the data that the user requests. A template is what allows you to greet a user based on the time of day, or a name that he/she enters. A static page cannot do this, because it will always be the same.

Templating engines (like Thymeleaf) are used to show data that is passed from the application, which may change depending on the user's interaction with the application.

QUESTIONS

1. What is a template?
   - a blueprint
   - a static page
   - a controller
   - a variable

2. What's a route?
   - a way to get home
   - a page request path
   - a url
   - a way to interpret a variable

3. What is the difference between GET and POST?
   - one is an action and other isn't
   - post is for sending data through email
   - get is for asking for things
   - get loads forms and post submits them

EXERCISE 1.01

Create an application called Exercise101_1 that displays the message - "Hello Welcome to Spring Boot Lesson 1" in a h2 tag.

1.02 USING A VARIABLE ON A TEMPLATE

LEARNING OBJECTIVES
- Passing a variable to the template from the controller
- Using the thymeleaf th:text attribute

THE WALKTHROUGH

1. **Create a Spring Boot Application**
   - Name it SpringBoot_102
   - Add the dependencies for the web and for thymeleaf
   - Hit next until you finish the wizard, and then wait until it's done.

2. **Create a Controller**
   - Right click on com.example.demo and click New -> Class
   - Name it HomeController.java
   - Edit it to look like this:

   ```
   @Controller
   public class HomeController {

       @RequestMapping("/")
       public String homePage(Model model){
           model.addAttribute("myvar", "Say hello to the people.");
           return "hometemplate";
       }
   }
   ```

3. **Create a Template**
   - Right click on templates and click New -> Html
   - Name it hometemplate.html
   - Edit it to look like this:

   ```
   <!DOCTYPE html>
   <html lang="en" xmlns:th="http://www.thymeleaf.org">
     <head>
       <meta charset="UTF-8" />
       <title>Title</title>
     </head>
     <body>
       <h2>Hello World!</h2>
       <p th:text="${myvar}"></p>
     </body>
   </html>
   ```

1.02 USING A VARIABLE ON A TEMPLATE

4. Run your application and open a browser, if you type in the URL http://localhost:8080 you should see Screen 1.02.1.

Hello World!

Say hello to the people

Screen 1.02.1

IMPORTS

CONTROLLER
`org.springframework.stereotype.Controller`

MODEL
`org.springframework.ui.Model`

REQUESTMAPPING
`org.springframework.web.bind.annotation.RequestMapping`

WHAT'S GOING ON

In the homePage method of the HomeController, we are passing data to the template.

An object named model, of class Model, is being passed as an argument to the homePage method. This will create a container that can hold as many objects that you put in it for use by your template. Think of it as a container that is passed between the controller and the view so that they can share objects.

The objects that the model holds are called attributes. This is why you add attributes to the model, using the model.addAttributes method. The arguments passed are the name you want the object to have (this is what your templates will call that object), and the actual object you want to make available.

In the above example, a string of value "Say hello to the people" is being passed to the model, and it is named "myvar". This is why "myvar" is being used in the template, and it displays the value that was assigned to it from the HomeController.

The "${}" in the template indicates that a variable is expected, and its value should be displayed. This is a Thymeleaf variable expression.

You are using this variable expression to tell the template that text should be displayed within the paragraph tag, and that the text should be the value of the object called myvar.

1.02 USING A VARIABLE ON A TEMPLATE

There is also static text in the HTML file - this is the Hello World text within the **<h2>** tags. It doesn't change at runtime. The user will see both types of text when the hometemplate file is displayed.

QUESTIONS

1. If you declared your controller method like this: `public String myVals(Model model)`, then how do you send a value to the template?
   - model.add("val", "greeting")
   - model.addAttribute("val", "greeting")
   - model.attribute("val","greeting")

2. If you successfully send a variable called "myvar" to the template, which of the following would work on the template?
   - `<div th:text="${myvar}"></div>`
   - `<div th:text="myvar"></div>`
   - `<div> th:text="${myvar}"</div>`
   - `<div "${myvar}"></div>`

EXERCISE 1.02

Create an application that passes two variables to the template and have the template display those values.

1.03 USING A PROPERTY VARIABLE ON A TEMPLATE

LEARNING OBJECTIVES
- Loading a value in the template from the messages.properties file

THE WALKTHROUGH

1. **Create a Spring Boot Application**
   - Name it SpringBoot_103
   - Add the dependencies for the web and for thymeleaf
   - Hit next until you finish the wizard, and then wait until it's done.

2. **Create a Controller**
   - Right click on com.example.demo and click New -> Class
   - Name it HomeController.java
   - Edit it to look like this:

   ```
   @Controller
   public class HomeController {

       @RequestMapping("/")
       public String homePage(){
           return "hometemplate";
       }
   }
   ```

3. **Create a Template**
   - Right click on templates and click New -> Html
   - Name it hometemplate.html
   - Edit it to look like this:

   ```
   <!DOCTYPE html>
   <html lang="en" xmlns:th="http://www.thymeleaf.org">
   <head>
       <meta charset="UTF-8" />
       <title>Title</title>
   </head>
   <body>
       <h2>Hello World!</h2>
       <p th:text="#{static.message}"></p>
   </body>
   </html>
   ```

1.03 USING A PROPERTY VARIABLE ON A TEMPLATE

4. **Create a messages.properties file**
   - Right click on resources and click New -> File
   - Name it messages.properties
   - Edit it to look like this:

   ```
   static.message=Hello World!
   ```

5. Run your application and open a browser, if you type in the URL http://localhost:8080 you should see something like *Screen 1.03.1*.

Screen 1.03.1

IMPORTS

CONTROLLER
`org.springframework.stereotype.Controller`

REQUESTMAPPING
`org.springframework.web.bind.annotation.RequestMapping`

WHAT'S GOING ON

The messages.properties file is where you will put all text that will be shown to users within your application. If you are translating text into other languages, you can create files for each language using the locale for that language, e.g. message_es.properties (for Spanish). This makes it easy to display text consistently across the application and also to create custom messages that can be used for validation errors.

The "#{}" in the template indicates that a pre-defined message should be displayed. This is a Thymeleaf message expression.

You are using this message expression to tell the template that text should be displayed within the paragraph tag, and that text should be the value that has been set for static.message in the message properties file (or the relevant locale file if the user chooses a different language).

1.03 USING A PROPERTY VARIABLE ON A TEMPLATE

Again, there is also static text in the HTML file - this is the Hello World text within the **<h2>** tags.

For more information about Thymeleaf expressions, see the "Thymeleaf Expression Sytnax" section of the link below:

http://www.thymeleaf.org/doc/articles/standarddialect5minutes.html

QUESTION

1. If you have an entry in your messages.properties that looks like: myval.name=Alton, which of the following would work on the template?
   - `<div th:text="#{myval}"></div>`
   - `<div th:text="#myval.name"></div>`
   - `<div> th:text="#{myval}"</div>`
   - `<div th:text="#{myval.name}"></div>`

EXERCISE 1.03

Create an application that passes the value "Hello World from Spring Boot" to the template from the messages.properties file.

ESSENTIAL TOOLS

2.01 Handling Form Values -- The Hard Way
2.02 Creating a Java Bean
2.03 Handling Form Values -- The Easy Way
2.04 Form Validation

2.01 HANDLING FORM VALUES -- THE HARD WAY

LEARNING OBJECTIVES
- Capturing form values in the controller
- Using the thymeleaf th:action attribute

THE WALKTHROUGH

1. **Create a Spring Boot Application**
   - Name it SpringBoot_201
   - Add the dependencies for the web and for thymeleaf
   - Hit next until you finish the wizard, and then wait until it's done.

2. **Create a Controller**
   - Right click on com.example.demo and click New -> Class
   - Name it HomeController.java
   - Edit it to look like this:

   ```
   @Controller
   public class HomeController {
       @RequestMapping("/loadform")
       public String loadFormPage(){
           return "formtemplate";
       }
       @RequestMapping("/processform")
       public String loadFromPage(@RequestParam("login") String login, Model model){
           model.addAttribute("loginval", login);
           return "confirm";
       }
   }
   ```

3. **Create a Template for the form**
   - Right click on templates and click New -> Html
   - Name it formtemplate.html
   - Edit the empty body tag (<body></body>) to look like this:

   ```
   <body>
   <form action="#" th:action="@{/processform}" method="post">
       Login: <input type="text" name="login" />
       <input type="submit" value="Submit" />
   </form>
   </body>
   ```

2.01 HANDLING FORM VALUES -- THE HARD WAY

4. **Create a Template for the confirmation**
   - Right click on templates and click New -> Html
   - Name it confirm.html
   - Edit the empty body tag (<body></body>) to look like this:

   ```
   <body>
       <p th:inline="text">
           The login used was [[${loginval}]].
       </p>
   </body>
   ```

5. Run your application and open a browser, if you type in the URL http://localhost:8080/loadform you should see *Screen 2.01.1*.

6. Once you enter a value and click submit, you should see a page that looks like *Screen 2.01.2*.

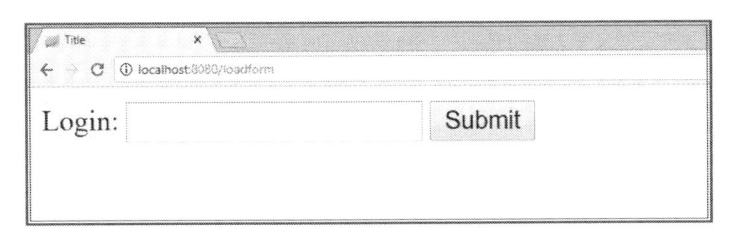

Screen 2.01.1

Screen 2.01.2

IMPORTS

CONTROLLER
`org.springframework.stereotype.Controller`

MODEL
`org.springframework.ui.Model`

REQUESTMAPPING
`org.springframework.web.bind.annotation.RequestMapping`

REQUESTPARAM
`org.springframework.web.bind.annotation.RequestParam`

WHAT'S GOING ON

The "/loadform" path displays the template formtemplate.html to the user.

The "/processform" path processes both get and post requests in the same way, so if you type http://localhost:8080/processform?login=Randomusername, you should see the same value as if you enter Randomusername in the login box displayed when you visit the "loadform" route.

The `th:action` attribute specifies what to do after you submit the data. It tells Spring Boot what endpoint to use to process the form's data.

2.01 HANDLING FORM VALUES -- THE HARD WAY

`@RequestParam` means that the loadFromPage method expects a parameter (either in the URL as a GET request, or posted to the form via a POST request) that is called login, and passes the value of that parameter to the model as "loginval". The html templates can now access the value of the login string as "loginval".

`th:inline` indicates that the value of text to be displayed is shown within the tag. To make sure the values of your Thymeleaf expresssions are evaluated, enclose your expressions in double square parentheses - [[ ]].

QUESTIONS

1. Which of the following tells thymeleaf what route to use to submit the form to?
   - th:object
   - th:action
   - th:text
   - th:field

2. Webpages are usually loaded using which HTML verb?
   - GET
   - PUT
   - POST
   - DELETE

3. Web forms are usually submitted using which HTML verb?
   - GET
   - PUT
   - POST
   - DELETE

EXERCISE 2.01

Create an application with two pages: the default page is a form asking for an email and when that page is submitted the user is sent to another page that outputs the email on the template

2.02 CREATING A JAVA BEAN

LEARNING OBJECTIVES
- Creating a Java Bean

THE WALKTHROUGH

1. **Create a Spring Boot Application**
   - Name it SpringBoot_202
   - Add the dependencies for the web and for thymeleaf
   - Hit next until you finish the wizard, and then wait until it's done.

2. **Create a Class**
   - Right click on com.example.demo and click New -> Class
   - Name it Song.java
   - Edit it to look like this:

   ```java
   public class Song {
       private long id;
       private String name;
       private String artist;
       private String album;
       private int rating;
       private int year;
   }
   ```

3. **Autogenerate getters and setters**
   - Right click on the word Song in the class declaration and select generate -> Getters and Setters
   - Select all the fields listed and click OK

WHAT'S GOING ON

You will use beans all the time in Java. To create one, you will need to create an ordinary class, add private member variables, and add public getter and setter methods to it. This class is going to be a blueprint for all of the objects created for that class. Every time you instantiate an object of the class (i.e. create a copy of the class you can actually use), you will use getters and setters to modify and access the values of the variables within the class.

2.02 CREATING A JAVA BEAN

QUESTIONS

1. Member variables of a Java Bean should be public?
   - True
   - False
   - Both
   - Neither

2. Getter and Setter methods of a Java Bean should be public?
   - True
   - False
   - Both
   - Neither

Exercise 2.02

Create an application with a Java Bean that represents a student. It should include fields for name, age, height and phone number. It should have private member variables and public getters and setters.

2.03 HANDLING FORM VALUES -- THE EASY WAY

LEARNING OBJECTIVES

- Retrieving values from a form using a Java Bean
- Using the thymeleaf th:object attribute
- Using the thymeleaf th:field attribute

THE WALKTHROUGH

1. **Create a Spring Boot Application**
   - Name it SpringBoot_203
   - Add the dependencies for the web and for thymeleaf
   - Hit next until you finish the wizard, and then wait until it's done.

2. **Create a Class**
   - Right click on com.example.demo and click New -> Java Class
   - Name it Song.java
   - Edit it to look like this:

   ```java
   public class Song {
       private long id;
       private String name;
       private String artist;
       private String album;
       private int rating;
       private int year; }
   ```

3. **Autogenerate getters and setters**
   - Inside your Song.java file, Right-click on the word Song and select generate -> Getters and Setters
   - Select all the fields listed and click OK

2.03 HANDLING FORM VALUES -- THE EASY WAY

4. **Create a Controller**
   - Right click on com.example.demo and click New -> Java Class
   - Name it HomeController.java
   - Edit it to look like this:

   ```
   @Controller
   public class HomeController {
       @GetMapping("/songform")
       public String loadFormPage(Model model){
           model.addAttribute("song", new Song());
           return "songform";
       }
       @PostMapping("/songform")
       public String loadFromPage(@ModelAttribute Song song, Model model) {
           model.addAttribute("song", song);
           return "confirmsong";
       }
   }
   ```

5. **Create a Template for the form**
   - Right click on templates and click New -> Html
   - Name it songform.html
   - Edit the empty body tag (<body></body>) to look like this:

   ```html
   <body><form action="#" th:action="@{/songform}" th:object="${song}" method="post">
       Name: <input type="text" th:field="*{name}" /><br />
       Artist: <input type="text" th:field="*{artist}" /><br />
       Album: <input type="text" th:field="*{album}" /><br />
       Rating: <input type="number" th:field="*{rating}" /><br />
       Year: <input type="number" th:field="*{year}" /><br />
       <input type="submit" value="Submit" />
   </form></body>
   ```

6. **Create a Template for the confirmation**
   - Right click on templates and click New -> Html
   - Name it confirmsong.html
   - Edit the empty body tag (<body></body>) to look like this:

   ```html
   <body>
       <p th:inline="text">The song name was [[${song.name}]].<br />
       The artist name is [[${song.artist}]].<br />
       The album name is [[${song.album}]].<br />
       The rating was [[${song.rating}]] and the year was [[${song.year}]].</p>
   </body>
   ```

2.03 HANDLING FORM VALUES -- THE EASY WAY

7. Run your application and open a browser, if you type in the URL http://localhost:8080/songform.
8. Once you enter a value and click submit, you should see the confirmation screen.

IMPORTS

CONTROLLER
`org.springframework.stereotype.Controller`

MODEL
`org.springframework.ui.Model`

GETMAPPING
`org.springframework.web.bind.annotation.GetMapping`

POSTMAPPING
`org.springframework.web.bind.annotation.PostMapping`

WHAT'S GOING ON

CONTROLLER

You are creating routes for both GET and POST requests to the songform endpoint ("/songform"). **@GetMapping** processes the GET requests, and **@PostMapping** processes post requests. In the loadFormPage method, you are adding a new instance of the Song class to the model. This creates an 'empty copy' of the Song class named "song", which can be accessed by the songform html template. When the user submits information to the form, it is kept within the model, and can be drawn down into the loadFromPage method using the @ModelAttribute annotation. This specifies that a model attribute of type Song which will be referred to as song in the method will be used. song is a Song object containing the values that were entered by the user into songform.html. "song" is now available to be used by confirmsong.html.

VIEW (HTML TEMPLATES)

songform.html: A form is being created to accept values from the user. Since you are accepting values from the user, when he/she clicks the submit button (the HTML element with input type="submit"), then the form values will be sent via a POST request to "/songform". This will access the loadFromPage method.

th:action indicates what should happen when the submit button is pressed. It uses a URL expression to indicate the route the user will be directed to in the controller.

th:object indicates that the form's values will be saved in the object called "song", which was passed from the controller.

th:field indicates that the value that is entered into an element corresponds to the value of the Song object referred to as song in the html template. When the form is posted, that value will be posted to the corresponding variable in the controller, and can also be accessed with getter methods if necessary. The input types show components that are best suited for capturing the selected type of information. For example, the number type will show a component that is best suited for increasing and decreasing integer values, while a text input will

2.03 HANDLING FORM VALUES -- THE EASY WAY

allow users to enter string values. *{} is a Thymeleaf selection expression that refers to a previously defined object, and indicates that all fields that are being referred to are from that object. In this case, the name, artist, album, rating and year fields all belong to the Song object called 'song' in the songform.html template.

confirmsong.html: When the user entered values into songform.html, and the Song object was populated with the values, it was passed to the loadFromPage method as part of a post request. The Song object was then passed to confirmsong.html, and is still accessible as "song". This means that song's values can be accessed in confirmsong.html. The getter and setter methods you created are used to read and modify the values of the Song object. For example, **[[${song.name}]]** calls the value of song.getName(), and displays it in the html field. Make sure you create getters and setters for each field, otherwise you will not be able to set or access values for the objects you create.

QUESTIONS

1. In this lesson, the Song class is not a Java Bean.
   - True
   - False

2. If you used the following code for your controller method, what would be the proper way to refer to the song's name in the thymeleaf?

   ```
   public String loadFormPage(Model model){
        model.addAttribute("jazzy", new Song());
        return "songform";
   }
   ```

   - th:text="${song.name}"
   - th:text="${Song.name}"
   - th:text="${jazzy.song.name}"
   - th:text="${jazzy.name}"

EXERCISE 2.03

Create an application that allows the user to input an employee object that is then reflected back to the user on the confirmation page. An employee object should include first name, last name, SSN and the DOB.

2.04 FORM VALIDATION

LEARNING OBJECTIVES

- Using form validation annotations in Spring Boot
- Checking for valid submissions in the controller
- Displaying validation messages on the template

THE WALKTHROUGH

1. **Create a Spring Boot Application**
   - Name it SpringBoot_204
   - Add the dependencies for the web and for thymeleaf
   - Hit next until you finish the wizard, and then wait until it's done.

2. **Create a Class**
   - Right click on com.example.demo and click New -> Class
   - Name it Tvshow.java
   - Edit it to look like this:

   ```
   public class Tvshow {
       @NotNull
       @Min(1)
       private long id;

       @NotNull
       @Size(min=3, max=20)
       private String name;

       @NotNull
       @Size(min=3, max=10)
       private String type;

       @NotNull
       @Size(min=10, max=30)
       private String description;
   }
   ```

3. **Autogenerate getters and setters**
   - Inside your Tvshow.java file, right-click on the word Tvshow and select generate -> Getters and Setters
   - Select all the fields list and click OK

2.04 FORM VALIDATION

4. **Create a Controller**
   - Right click on com.example.demo and click New -> Class
   - Name it HomeController.java
   - Edit it to look like this:

   ```
   @Controller
   public class HomeController {
       @GetMapping("/tvform")
       public String loadTvForm(Model model){
           model.addAttribute("tvshow", new Tvshow());
           return "tvform";
       }

       @PostMapping("/tvform")
       public String processTvForm(@Valid Tvshow tvshow,
           BindingResult result){
           if (result.hasErrors()){
               return "tvform";
           }
           return "tvshowconfirm";
       }
   }
   ```

5. **Create a Template for the form**
   - Right click on templates and click New -> Html
   - Name it tvform.html
   - Edit your empty body tags *<body></body>* to look like this:

   ```html
   <body>
       <form action="#"
             th:action="@{/tvform}"
             th:object="${tvshow}"
             method="post">
           Id :<input type="number" th:field="*{id}" />
           <span th:if="${#fields.hasErrors('id')}"
                 th:errors="*{id}"></span><br />
           Name :<input type="text" th:field="*{name}" />
           <span th:if="${#fields.hasErrors('name')}"
                 th:errors="*{name}"></span><br />
           Type :<input type="text" th:field="*{type}" />
           <span th:if="${#fields.hasErrors('type')}"
                 th:errors="*{type}"></span><br />
           Description :<textarea rows="3" th:field="*{description}" />
           <span th:if="${#fields.hasErrors('description')}"
                 th:errors="*{description}"></span><br />
           <input type="submit" value="Submit" />
       </form>
   </body>
   ```

2.04 FORM VALIDATION

6. **Create a Template for the confirmation**
   - Right click on templates and click New -> Html
   - Name it tvshowconfirm.html
   - Edit your empty body tags *<body></body>* to look like this:

   ```
   <body>
   <p th:inline="text">
       The tv show's name was [[${tvshow.name}]].<br />
       It is a [[${tvshow.type}]].<br />
       It could be best described as
       [[${tvshow.description}]].
   </p>
   </body>
   ```

7. Run your application and open a browser, if you type in the URL http://localhost:8080/tvform you should see *Screen 2.04.1*.

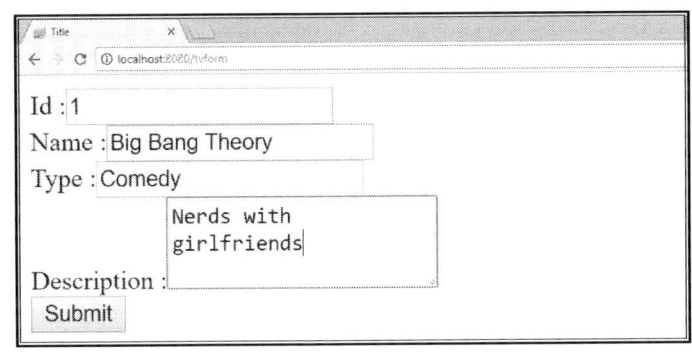

Screen 2.04.1

8. If you enter values that violate your constraints and try to submit the form, it will show you an error like in *Screen 2.04.2*. But once you enter valid values and click submit, you should see a page that looks like *Screen 2.04.3*.

Screen 2.04.2

Screen 2.04.3

2.04 FORM VALIDATION

IMPORTS

BINDINGRESULT
`org.springframework.validation.BindingResult`

CONTROLLER
`org.springframework.stereotype.Controller`

GETMAPPING
`org.springframework.web.bind.annotation.GetMapping`

MIN
`javax.validation.constraints.Min`

MODEL
`org.springframework.ui.Model`

NOTNULL
`javax.validation.constraints.NotNull`

POSTMAPPING
`org.springframework.web.bind.annotation.PostMapping`

SIZE
`javax.validation.constraints.Size`

WHAT'S GOING ON

A bean for TvShow is being created, and it includes constraint annotations. These constrains restrict the values that can be assigned to the variables. Remember the getters and setters!

CONSTRAINTS AND VALIDATION

`@NotNull` and `@Min(1)` ensure that the user enters a value into this field. You can also indicate that the input is valid for a range of a number of characters - e.g. there should be a minimum of 3 characters and a maximum of 30 for the name of the TV show.

CONTROLLER

There are two routes mapped out in this controller - one each for get and post requests to "/tvform". The get request creates an empty object to be passed to tvform.html, so that a user can enter information about TV shows. The post request validates the input received according to the annotations in the bean. If values entered are invalid, tvform.html will be displayed with the default error messages for the errors encountered. If the values entered are valid, tvshowconfirm.html will be shown.

VIEW - TVFORM.HTML

As in the previous example, the entries made by the user are being put into an object that is created in the controller and passed to the html form. This object is referred to as "tvshow" in tvform.html. Once the user clicks the "Submit" button, the information is posted to the route indicated by the th:action form attribute. The input fields are also being validated based on the annotations in the bean.

`th:if="${#fields.hasErrors('id')}"` gets the return values from BindingResult, and `th:errors = "*{id}"` builds the default error message for the field if there are errors.

2.04 FORM VALIDATION

QUESTIONS

1. What annotation indicates only that the field cannot be blank?
   - @NotNull
   - @Min(1)
   - @Size(min=1, max=30)
   - @NotBlank

2. What annotation indicates that the numeric field must be greater than 0?
   - @NotZero
   - @Min(1)
   - @Size(min=1)
   - @NotNull

3. What annotation indicates that the string field must have more than 0 characters? (Select all that apply)
   - @NotNull
   - @Min(1)
   - @Size(min=1)
   - @NotZero

EXERCISE 2.04

Create an application that has a Car Java Bean that includes name, type and description as attributes. The application should use a form to populate that bean and show a confirmation page the displays which values were entered on the form.

3.0 DATA TOOLS

3.01 Saving Data to a Database

3.02 Looping through a list with Thymeleaf in Spring Boot

3.03 Complete Data Lifecycle - form, list, detail, delete

3.04 Automatically Adding Records to the Database When Your Application Runs

3.05 Database Relationships - Many to Many

3.06 Database Relationships - One to Many

3.07 Database Relationships - One to One

3.01 SAVING DATA TO THE DATABASE

LEARNING OBJECTIVES
- Adding database support in Spring Boot
- Using the H2 Database
- Using database annotations - @Id, @GeneratedValue, and @Entity
- Configuring your application to use H2 Console

THE WALKTHROUGH

1. **Create a Spring Boot Application**
   - Name it SpringBoot_301
   - Add the dependencies for the web and thymeleaf.
   - Select the dependencies for devtools, jpa and h2.
     - **On the left column click on Developer Tools and then click the checkbox next to Spring Boot Dev Tools in the middle column**
     - **On the left column click on SQL and then click the checkboxes next to Spring Data JPA and H2 Database in the middle column**
     - **Click the Next button in the lower right hand corner**
   - Hit next until you finish the wizard, and then wait until it's done.

2. **Create a Class**
   - Right click on com.example.demo and click New -> Class
   - Name it Person.java
   - Edit it to look like this:

   ```
   @Entity
   public class Person {
       @Id
       @GeneratedValue(strategy = GenerationType.AUTO)
       private long id;
       private String firstName;
       private String lastName;
   }
   ```

3. **Autogenerate getters and setters**
   - Inside your Person.java file, right-click on the word Person and select generate -> Getters and Setters
   - Select all the fields list and click OK

3.01 SAVING DATA TO THE DATABASE

4. **Configure H2**
   - Open application.properties
   - Edit it to look like this:
     ```
     spring.h2.console.enabled=true
     spring.h2.console.path=/h2-console
     spring.jpa.hibernate.ddl-auto=create
     spring.datasource.url = jdbc:h2:mem:testdb
     ```

5. Run your application and open a browser, if you type in the URL http://localhost:8080/h2-console you should see *Screen 3.01.1*.

6. **Fix the JDBC URL (if you need to...)**
   - Change the JDBC URL to jdbc:h2:mem:testdb (if it isn't that already)
   - Click connect and you should see *Screen 3.01.2*.

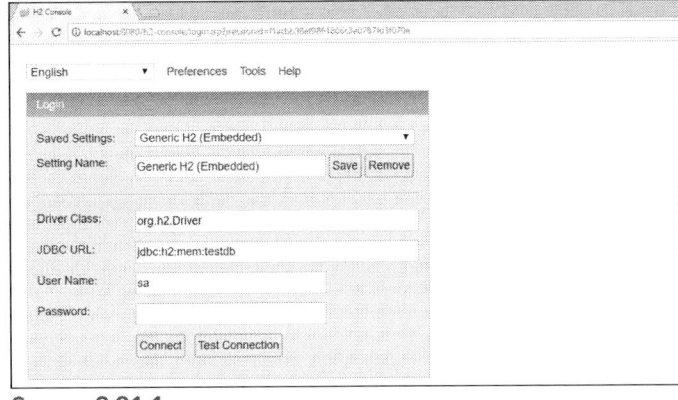

Screen 3.01.1

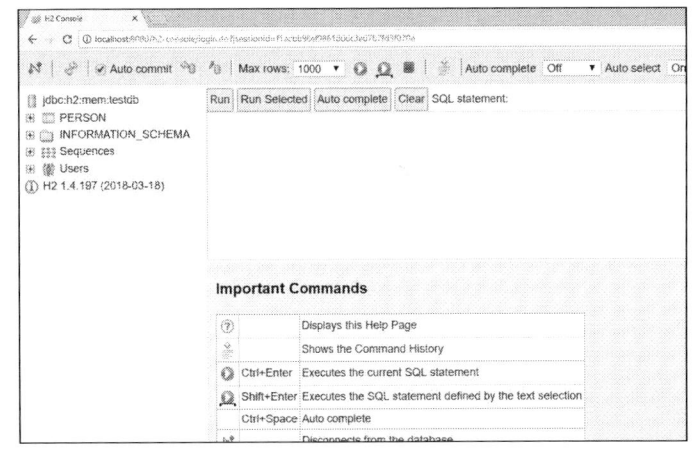

Screen 3.01.2

IMPORTS

ENTITY
    javax.persistence.Entity

GENERATED VALUE
    javax.persistence.GeneratedValue

GENERATIONTYPE
    javax.persistence.GenerationType

ID
    javax.persistence.Id

3.01 SAVING DATA TO THE DATABASE

WHAT'S GOING ON

You are creating a Spring Boot application that uses an in-memory database called H2 to store its data. If you create an application with the correct dependencies, you do not need to download additional software. Everything the application needs to run will be included when Maven downloads and includes the dependencies your application needs to work with.

CONTROLLER

Start by creating a class that uses the `@Entity` annotation to create a table in your database. The database in which the table will be located is determined by the application properties.

The fields in the Person class determine what data types will be used to store the data in the database, and also what kind of constraints will be used to ensure only valid data is stored.

The constraints are denoted by annotations. A list of annotations that can be used is listed in the Appendix.

The annotations being used on the Person class are as follows: `@Id` - this indicates that the field is the unique identifier that will be used for each row in the database. `@GeneratedValue` - this indicates that the identifier will be generated, and `strategy=GenerationType.AUTO` means a unique number will automatically be assigned to each row.

Remember the getters and setters! They are used to save and retrieve data to and from the database.

APPLICATION PROPERTIES

If you look inside the application.properties file (which can be found in the resources folder), you will find a number of settings that helps your application run properly. In this application, we were using it to configure the database..

`spring.h2.console.enabled=true` permits access to the database outside the application (using the h2 console).

`spring.h2.console.path=/h2-console` allows you to browse to the database to view the data in it by typing http://localhost:8080/h2-console. If your server port is not 8080, you will have to modify the path accordingly.

`spring.jpa.hibernate.ddl-auto=create` This allows the application to create database tables. In this mode, every time you run the application, it will create tables to store the data if they do not already exist. If the tables already exist, all data will be cleared, and any data you enter will last until you restart the application.

`spring.datasource.url=...` This specifies the url of the connected database.

3.01 SAVING DATA TO THE DATABASE

QUESTIONS

1. if your application.properties file looks like the following, what will be the url where you can access the console for the h2 database?

   ```
   spring.h2.console.enabled=true
   spring.h2.console.path=/myh2
   spring.jpa.hibernate.ddl-auto=create
   ```

   - http://localhost:8080/h2
   - http://localhost:8080/h2-console
   - http://localhost:8080/myh2
   - http://localhost:8080/h2_console

2. When using H2 as an in-memory database, when you restart your application your data:
   - persists
   - is wiped
   - is saved on github
   - can be recovered using Maven

EXERCISE 3.01

Create an application that defines a Dog class that includes fields for id, name and age. It should include the proper annotations to make the name required and make the minimum age 1.

3.02 LOOPING THROUGH A LIST WITH THYMELEAF

LEARNING OBJECTIVES
- Creating a CrudRepository
- Using Autowiring
- Passing lists of objects to a template
- Looping through a list object in Thymeleaf

THE WALKTHROUGH

1. **Create a Spring Boot Application**
   - Name it SpringBoot_302
   - Add the dependencies for web, thymeleaf, jpa and h2
   - Hit next until you finish the wizard, and then wait until it's done.

2. **Create a Class**
   - Right click on com.example.demo and click New -> Class
   - Name it Job.java
   - Edit it to look like this:

   ```
   @Entity
   public class Job {
       @Id
       @GeneratedValue(strategy = GenerationType.AUTO)
       private long id;

       @NotNull
       @Size(min=4)
       private String title;

       @NotNull
       @Size(min=3)
       private String employer;

       @NotNull
       @Size(min=10)
       private String description;
   }
   ```

3. **Autogenerate getters and setters**
   - Inside your Job.java file, right-click on the word Job and select generate -> Getters and Setters
   - Select all the fields list and click OK

3.02 LOOPING THROUGH A LIST WITH THYMELEAF

4. **Create a Repository**
   - Right click on com.example.demo and click New -> Class
   - Name it JobRepository.java
   - Edit it to look like this:

   ```
   public interface JobRepository extends CrudRepository<Job, Long> {
   }
   ```

5. **Create a Controller**
   - Right click on com.example.demo and click New -> Class
   - Name it HomeController.java
   - Edit it to look like this:

   ```
   @Controller
   public class HomeController {

       @Autowired
       JobRepository jobRepository;

       @RequestMapping("/")
       public String listJobs(Model model){
           model.addAttribute("jobs", jobRepository.findAll());
           return "list";
       }

       @GetMapping("/add")
       public String jobForm(Model model){
           model.addAttribute("job", new Job());
           return "jobform";
       }

       @PostMapping("/process")
       public String processForm(@Valid Job job, BindingResult result){
           if (result.hasErrors()){
               return "jobform";
           }
           jobRepository.save(job);
           return "redirect:/";
       }
   }
   ```

3.02 LOOPING THROUGH A LIST WITH THYMELEAF

6. **Create a Template for the form**
   - Right click on templates and click New -> Html
   - Name it jobform.html
   - Edit it the empty body tag (<body></body>) to look like this:

   ```
   <body>
   <h1>Job Form</h1>
   <form action="#" th:action="@{/process}" th:object="${job}" method="post">
       Title :<input type="text" th:field="*{title}" />
       <span th:if="${#fields.hasErrors('title')}"
           th:errors="*{title}"></span><br />
       Employer :<input type="text" th:field="*{employer}" />
       <span th:if="${#fields.hasErrors('employer')}"
           th:errors="*{employer}"></span><br />
       Description :<textarea rows="3" th:field="*{description}" />
       <span th:if="${#fields.hasErrors('description')}"
           th:errors="*{description}"></span>
       <br />
       <input type="submit" value="Submit" />
   </form>
   </body>
   ```

7. **Create a Template for the job listings**
   - Right click on templates and click New -> Html
   - Name it list.html
   - Edit it to look like this:

   ```
   <body>
   <h1>Job Form</h1>
   <a href="/add">Add a Job</a><br />
   <div th:each="job : ${jobs}">
       <h4 th:inline="text">[[${job.title}]] @ [[${job.employer}]]</h4>
       <p th:text="${job.description}"></p>
   </div>
   </body>
   ```

8. **Run your application and open a browser, if you type in the URL http://localhost:8080/add you should see *Screen 3.02.1*.**

9. **If you enter values and submit the form, it will show you a list of all the jobs added so far. So, you should see a page that looks like *Screen 3.02.2*.**

3.02 LOOPING THROUGH A LIST WITH THYMELEAF

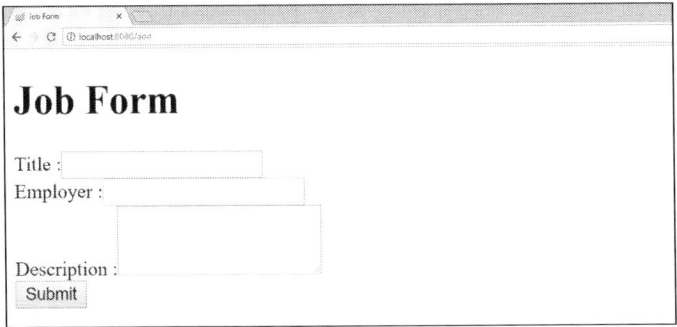

Screen 3.02.1

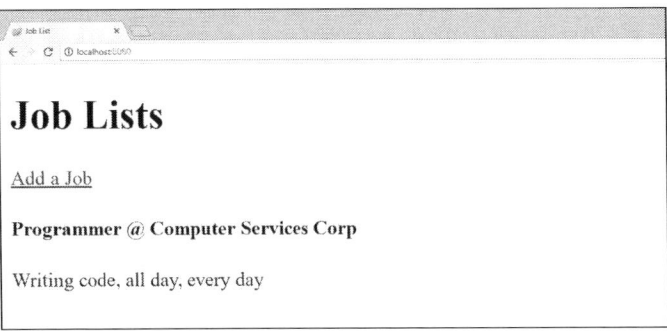

Screen 3.02.2

IMPORTS

AUTOWIRED
org.springframework.beans.factory.annotation.Autowired

BINDINGRESULT
org.springframework.validation.BindingResult

CONTROLLER
org.springframework.stereotype.Controller

CRUDREPOSITORY
org.springframework.data.repository.CrudRepository

ENTITY
javax.persistence.Entity

GENERATED VALUE
javax.persistence.GeneratedValue

GENERATIONTYPE
javax.persistence.GenerationType

GETMAPPING
org.springframework.web.bind.annotation.GetMapping

ID
javax.persistence.Id

MODEL
org.springframework.ui.Model

NOTNULL
javax.validation.constraints.NotNull

POSTMAPPING
org.springframework.web.bind.annotation.PostMapping

REQUESTMAPPING
org.springframework.web.bind.annotation.RequestMapping

SIZE
javax.validation.constraints.Size

WHAT'S GOING ON

You are using an in-memory database to store information about jobs. This information is captured from a user (or users) via an HTML form. The process is the same as for any other database (MySQL, Postgres, SQL Server, etc.), and you benefit from The Java Persistence API's ability to 'talk to' many different databases using the same Spring Boot code.

3.02 LOOPING THROUGH A LIST WITH THYMELEAF

MODEL

The Job Class

You are creating a class that will become a table in the H2 database. The annotations being used will determine how your application interacts with the database (e.g. automatically generating the Id which is used as the primary key for that table), and what kind of information the database stores in each field.

The Job Repository

This acts as your 'pipeline' to the database. The Job Repository has in-built methods that you can use to save, locate, and delete data. The Job Repository can return single or multiple instances of the jobs that are in the database, depending on the criteria used to locate fields.

CONTROLLER

This is where the action happens. Routes are mapped out for each action - Creating, Reading, Updating and Deleting data (CRUD).

What does `@Autowired` do?

When you create an instance of an object, you use the format `ObjectClass someObject = new ObjectClass();` This creates an instance of the object, and you can use it within the method where it is called. For JobRepository, that would mean that you had to instantiate the object within each method that used the JobReposity class, but that would be a pain. @Autowired tells the compiler to instantiate the repository object when the application runs, so you don't have to type out that line so many times!

`@RequestMapping("/")`

When a user visits the default route (e.g. http://localhost:8080), the user will see a list of records that have been saved in the database. This is because the Job Repository is being used to retrieve all available records, and the result of this search is being passed to the view (in an Iterable object called 'jobs'). The view will display the individual elements of the 'jobs' object using a Thymeleaf loop.

`@GetMapping("/add")`

When a user visits the default route (e.g. http://localhost:8080), a new and empty instance of the Job class will be created. This will be passed to the view (where it is referred to as 'job'), so that the user's input can be stored in fields within that model, and validated according to the rules set in the Job class.

`@PostMapping("/process")`

When a user presses the "submit" button, the view returns to the controller to execute the method under this route. This method checks the object that was passed to the view. That object is now populated with the

3.02 LOOPING THROUGH A LIST WITH THYMELEAF

user's input, which can be validated against the rules in the Job class. The **@Valid** annotation is used with the BindingResult object to check the object for validity according to the validation constraints.

If the user has entered invalid data, the input form will be entered with prompts each invalid field input, for the user to enter valid values. Once the user enters valid information for all required inputs, the controller will return to the default route.

"redirect" is being used to call a route. Note that if you use Model to create a model attribute, the job object that has been created and made available to the controller will disappear. In this case, ONLY use redirects for routes that support GET mapping.

VIEW

Remember when we edited the HTML template in lesson 1.00 to include the thymeleaf XML namespace? This allows you to use thymeleaf attributes in the HTML template.

jobform.html

This form serves two purposes. It accepts information from the user, and also informs the user about invalid data that was entered after the form has been submitted. When a new (and empty) object is passed to it, the form ignores the error messages, because the th:if statements evaluate to false. When an error occurs, the errors captured in the BindingResult object are passed back to the form, and checked for using

`${#fields.hasErrors('fieldname')}`

, where fieldname is the name of the field into which data was entered. If the th:if statement evaluates to true, then the span will display the default (or modified) error for that field:

`th:errors="*{title}"`

Remember

The form action uses a thymeleaf statement, th:action. This maps to a named route in the controller. The method used is POST, since information will be submitted to the application. Since th:action is being used, the form action is not required. If you still wish to use it, assign "#" to the form action.

list.html

This is where the items that were entered show up in the application. The object that was passed to the view "jobs" is looped through. This object is like a list, or array list, and contains a number of objects.

The th:each Thymeleaf statement is used to loop through the data. This can be confusing at first, but it is easier to understand if you think about it as an enhanced for loop.

3.02 LOOPING THROUGH A LIST WITH THYMELEAF

If you were looping through a similar object in the controller, you would do it this way:

```
Iterable <Job> jobs = jobRepository.findAll();
for(Job job:jobs)
{
 System.out.println(job.getTitle()+" @ "+job.getEmployer());
 System.out.println(job.getDescription());
}
```

In Thymeleaf, you are changing this slightly. The controller has already passed jobs to Thyemleaf. So now, the view has to iterate through it using th:each.

```html
<div th:each="job : ${jobs}">
    <h4 th:inline="text">[[${job.title}]] @ [[${job.employer}]]</h4>
    <p th:text="${job.description}"></p>
</div>
```

Note that the getters in Thymeleaf look like the variables declared in the Job class. They actually call the getters .getTitle(), .getEmployer(), and .getDescription() in the background to retrieve their values and display them in Thymeleaf. This is one of the most important reasons to add your getters and setters! If you don't, your application will throw an error while trying to render the Thymeleaf view.

QUESTIONS

```html
<div th:each="s  : ${students}">
```

1. If your template has code that looks like the above, which of the following would be the proper html code to use on your template to display the name attribute of the variable?
   - <h2 th:text="${students.name}"></h2>
   - <h2 th:text="${student.name}"></h2>
   - <h2 th:text="${s.name}"></h2>
   - <h2 th:inline="${s.name}"></h2>

EXERCISE 3.02

Create a Todo list application that has a class that stores the id, task name, due date and priority of each Todo item. Create a template that shows a list of all the Todo items in the database.

3.03 COMPLETE DATA LIFECYCLE - FORM, LIST, DETAIL, DELETE

LEARNING OBJECTIVES

- Creating a CrudRepository
- Passing lists of objects to a template
- Looping through a list object in Thymeleaf

THE WALKTHROUGH

1. **Create a Spring Boot Application**
   - Name it SpringBoot_303
   - Add the dependencies for web, thymeleaf, jpa and h2
   - Hit next until you finish the wizard, and then wait until it's done.

2. **Create a Class**
   - Right click on com.example.demo and click New -> Class
   - Name it Course.java
   - Edit it to look like this:

   ```
   @Entity
   public class Course {

       @Id
       @GeneratedValue(strategy = GenerationType.AUTO)
       private long id;

       @NotNull
       @Size(min=4)
       private String title;

       @NotNull
       @Size(min=3)
       private String instructor;

       @NotNull
       @Size(min=10)
       private String description;

       @NotNull
       @Min(3)
       private int credit;
   }
   ```

3. **Autogenerate getters and setters**
   - Inside your Course.java file, right-click on the word Course and select generate -> Getters and Setters
   - Select all the fields list and click OK

3.03 COMPLETE DATA LIFECYCLE - FORM, LIST, DETAIL, DELETE

4. **Create a Repository**
   - Right click on com.example.demo and click New -> Class
   - Name it CourseRepository.java
   - Edit it to look like this:

   ```
   public interface CourseRepository extends CrudRepository<Course, Long>{}
   ```

5. **Create a Controller**
   - Right click on com.example.demo and click New -> Class
   - Name it HomeController.java
   - Edit it to look like this:

   ```
   @Controller
   public class HomeController {

       @Autowired
       CourseRepository courseRepository;

       @RequestMapping("/")
       public String listCourses(Model model){
           model.addAttribute("courses", courseRepository.findAll());
           return "list";
       }

       @GetMapping("/add")
       public String courseForm(Model model){
           model.addAttribute("course", new Course());
           return "courseform";
       }

       @PostMapping("/process")
       public String processForm(@Valid Course course,
         BindingResult result){
           if (result.hasErrors()){
               return "courseform";
           }
           courseRepository.save(course);
           return "redirect:/";
       }

       @RequestMapping("/detail/{id}")
       public String showCourse(@PathVariable("id") long id, Model model)
       {
           model.addAttribute("course", courseRepository.findById(id).get());
           return "show";
       }
   ```

3.03 COMPLETE DATA LIFECYCLE - FORM, LIST, DETAIL, DELETE

```java
    @RequestMapping("/update/{id}")
    public String updateCourse(@PathVariable("id") long id,
            Model model){
        model.addAttribute("course", courseRepository.findById(id).get());
        return "courseform";
    }

    @RequestMapping("/delete/{id}")
    public String delCourse(@PathVariable("id") long id){
        courseRepository.deleteById(id);
        return "redirect:/";
    }
}
```

6. **Create a Template for the form**
   - Right click on templates and click New -> Html
   - Name it courseform.html
   - Edit the empty body tag (<body></body>) to look like this:

```html
<body>
<h1>Course Form</h1>
<form action="#" th:action="@{/process}" th:object="${course}" method="post">
    <input type="hidden" th:field="*{id}" />
    Title :<input type="text" th:field="*{title}" />
    <span th:if="${#fields.hasErrors('title')}"
          th:errors="*{title}"></span><br />
    Instructor :<input type="text" th:field="*{instructor}" />
    <span th:if="${#fields.hasErrors('instructor')}"
          th:errors="*{instructor}"></span><br />
    Description :<textarea rows="3" th:field="*{description}" />
    <span th:if="${#fields.hasErrors('description')}"
          th:errors="*{description}"></span><br />
    Credits :<input type="text" th:field="*{credit}" />
    <span th:if="${#fields.hasErrors('credit')}"
          th:errors="*{credit}"></span><br />
    <br />
    <input type="submit" value="Submit" />
</form>
</body>
```

7. **Create a Template for the course listings**
   - Right click on templates and click New -> Html
   - Name it list.html
   - Edit the empty body tag (<body></body>) to look like this:

3.03 COMPLETE DATA LIFECYCLE - FORM, LIST, DETAIL, DELETE

```html
<body>
<h1>Course List</h1>
<a href="/add">Add a Course</a><br />
<table>
    <tr>
        <th>Title</th>
        <th>Instructor</th>
        <th>Credits</th>
        <td>Actions</td>
    </tr>
    <tr th:each="course : ${courses}">
        <td th:text="${course.title}"></td>
        <td th:text="${course.instructor}"></td>
        <td th:text="${course.credit}"></td>
        <td>
            <a th:href="@{/update/{id}(id=${course.id})}">Update</a> -
            <a th:href="@{/detail/{id}(id=${course.id})}">Details</a> -
            <a th:href="@{/delete/{id}(id=${course.id})}">Delete</a>
        </td></tr>
</table>
</body>
```

8. **Create a template for course detail**
   - Right click on templates and click New -> Html
   - Name it show.html
   - Edit the empty body tag (<body></body>) to look like this::

   ```html
   <body>
   <a href="/">Show All Courses</a><br />
     Title :<span th:text="${course.title}" ></span><br />
     Instructor :<span th:text="${course.instructor}" ></span><br />
     Description :<p th:text="${course.description}" ></p>
     Credits :<span th:text="${course.credit}" ></span><br />
     <a th:href="@{/delete/{id}(id=${course.id})}">Delete this course</a>
   </body>
   ```

9. **Configure H2 to use the console**
   - Configure H2
   - Open application.properties
   - Edit it to look like this:

   ```
   spring.h2.console.enabled=true
   spring.h2.console.path=/h2-console
   spring.jpa.hibernate.ddl-auto=create
   spring.datasource.url=jdbc:h2:mem:testdb
   ```

3.03 COMPLETE DATA LIFECYCLE - FORM, LIST, DETAIL, DELETE

10. Run your application and open a browser, if you type in the URL http://localhost:8080/add you should see *Screen 3.03.1*.

11. If you enter values and submit the form, it will show you a list of all the jobs added so far. So, you should see a page that looks like *Screen 3.03.2*.

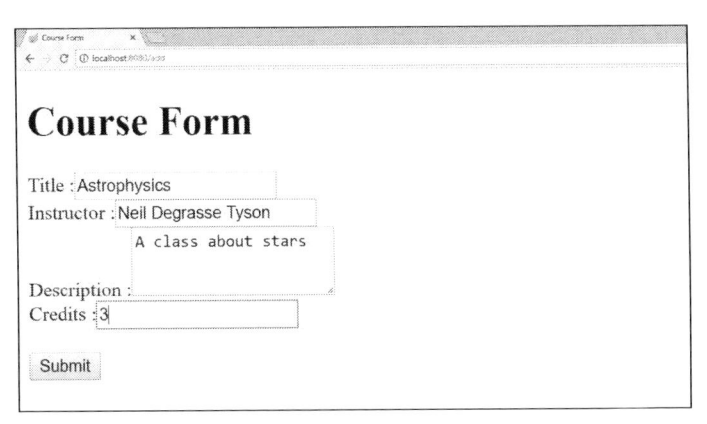

Screen 3.03.1

Screen 3.03.2

IMPORTS

AUTOWIRED
org.springframework.beans.factory.annotation.Autowired

BINDINGRESULT
org.springframework.validation.BindingResult

CONTROLLER
org.springframework.stereotype.Controller

CRUDREPOSITORY
org.springframework.data.repository.CrudRepository

ENTITY
javax.persistence.Entity

GENERATED VALUE
javax.persistence.GeneratedValue

GENERATIONTYPE
javax.persistence.GenerationType

GETMAPPING
org.springframework.web.bind.annotation.GetMapping

ID
javax.persistence.Id

MIN
javax.validation.constraints.Min

MODEL
org.springframework.ui.Model

NOTNULL
javax.validation.constraints.NotNull

PATHVARIABLE
org.springframework.web.bind.annotation.PathVariable

POSTMAPPING
org.springframework.web.bind.annotation.PostMapping

REQUESTMAPPING
org.springframework.web.bind.annotation.RequestMapping

SIZE
javax.validation.constraints.Size

3.03 COMPLETE DATA LIFECYCLE - FORM, LIST, DETAIL, DELETE

WHAT'S GOING ON

Congratulations on your first 'full' application! You can now add data to the database, as well as review, modify and delete it.

MODEL

The **@Entity** annotation tells your application that a table should be created in your database that has fields named after the variables in the class. Depending on the database you are using, the data types may have slightly different names, but they will be the best types for the kind of data you are working with, so you don't have to think about how the data is stored and retrieved. Finaly, remember your getters and setters!

The annotations for validation should be familiar - these are used to determine whether the information input by the user is what is expected by the applicaition. If so, the data can be stored. If not, the view will indicate to the user where the problems are (for details, see the 'View' section), so they can be corrected.

CrudRepository

This acts as a pipeline to your database, automatically storing, modifying, and retrieving data. Through the methods that CrudRepository makes available to you, you can instantly save, find one or all, and delete records by using very simple methods.

CONTROLLER

This is where the action happens. Routes are mapped out for each action - Creating, Reading, Updating and Deleting data (CRUD).

Default Route ("/")

When the user visits this route, the user will see a list of all the course entries that have been made. This is because the model contains the result of the .findAll() method, which pulls all the data for a selected model from the database. This data is made available to the view as a variable named ("courses").

Add route ("/add")

When a user visits this route, a new instance of the Courses class will be created and passed to the view. This will hold all values that the user enters into the form and return them to the controller at the route specified on the form by the POST method.

Process route ("/process")

This route validates the course for errors, saves it to the database (using the Course- Repository object created by the **@Autowired** annotation), and redirects the user to the default route.

3.03 COMPLETE DATA LIFECYCLE - FORM, LIST, DETAIL, DELETE

Update route ("/update/{id}")

When a user wants to modify a record, that user can retrieve the details of that record by opening up http://localhost/8080/update, and adding the ID of the user whose record is being modified. The {id} parameter in this case is a primary key that exists in the database, because there should be only one record that matches this criterion.

The .findById() method is used to pull up that record, and it is passed to the view as an object named "course".

Delete

The delete route follows the same pattern, but instead of showing the record, it is immediately deleted from the database. When the user is re-directed to the default route, this will show in the list that is displayed, as that record will not be shown in the list.

VIEWS

This is an introduction to parameterised thymeleaf URLs. Sometimes you want to pass additional information to a URL so that you can perform operations on data. This option allows you to add parameters to a route, so that the values that are passed can be used in your controller. You determine what these values are, and how they are processed.

courseform.html

This is the form that allows users to add new courses. It is tied to the course model (**th:object="${course}"**), and has validation that uses the default error messaging for the fields that have been annotated in the model (e.g. title and instructor).

list.html

This template uses a thymeleaf loop (th:each) to show the details of each course that is passed in the courses object (a collection of course items) from the default route.

It also includes links for updating, showing details of, and deleting listed courses using URL PARAMETERS - so you have the potential to access all your CRUD (Create Read Update Delete) operations in one form. The user will be re-directed to different routes when he/she clicks each link. Each one will allow the user to carry out the selected CRUD operation. It also allows users to add a new course by clicking the appropriate link towards the top of the page.

show.html

This shows information for a single course, and has an option to delete the course, using its id as a PARAMETER in the route to delete the item.

3.03 COMPLETE DATA LIFECYCLE - FORM, LIST, DETAIL, DELETE

EXERCISE 3.03

Create a Todo list application that has a class that stores the id, task name, due date and priority of each Todo item. Create templates and controller end points to handle creating, updating and deleting Todo items. Also, create an endpoint that handles listing all the Todo items.

3.04 AUTOMATICALLY ADDING RECORDS TO YOUR DATABASE

LEARNING OBJECTIVES
- Implementing a function to autoload data on application start

WALKTHROUGH

1. Take your existing application from Lesson 3.03
2. Add loaded constructor to Course
   - Edit the Course.java file
   - Right-click the word Course and Select Generate -> Constructor
   - Click on title, instructor, description, credit
   - Click OK
3. Add default constructor to Course
   - Edit the Course.java file
   - Right-click the word Course and Select Generate -> Constructor
   - Click on the "Select None" button
4. Add a DataLoader Class
   - Right-click on com.example.demo and click New -> Class
   - Name it DataLoader.java
   - Edit the contents to look like this:

```
@Component
public class DataLoader implements CommandLineRunner {

  @Autowired
  CourseRepository repository;

  @Override
  public void run(String... strings) throws Exception{
    Course course;
    course = new Course("Astrophysics", "Neil D Tyson", "Just a course on stars", 3);
    repository.save(course);

    course = new Course("Calculus", "Carol Henley",
        "Rate of Change of the Rate of Change", 3);
    repository.save(course);

    course = new Course("Freshman English", "Geraldine Pegram",
        "Learn your language children", 3);
    repository.save(course);
  }
}
```

3.04 AUTOMATICALLY ADDING RECORDS TO YOUR DATABASE

5. Run your application and open a browser, if you type in the URL http://localhost:8080 and you should see *Screen 3.04.1*.
6. Assuming your dataloader implements CommandLineRunner, you can use this as a template for how you would implement this type of functionality in your own applications.

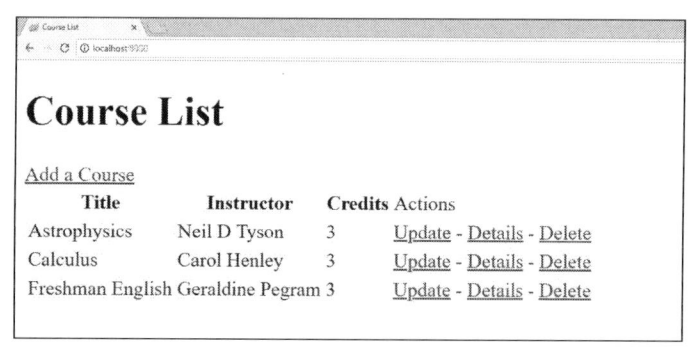

Screen 3.04.1

WHAT'S GOING ON

Implementing a Data Loader is fairly simple. You have to create the run method Override and include all the code that you need to insert data into your tables. The class doesn't need to be called DataLoader, but it does have to have the **@Component** annotation and it must implement CommandLineRunner.

If you do everything properly, then everytime your program executes, after it creates the tables, it will run your insert commands to add data to the database. It doesn't matter how quickly someone tries to load the web site, the code in the Command Line Runner will occur first.

QUESTIONS

```
@Component
```

1. If the above code is in your file called MyRunner.java, which of the following lines would be used to make the contents run before the website becomes available.
    - `public class DataLoader`
    - `public class DataLoader implements CommandLineRunner`
    - `public class MyRunner`
    - `public class MyRunner implements CommandLineRunner`

3.04 AUTOMATICALLY ADDING RECORDS TO YOUR DATABASE

2. Once you have created your data loader class which of the following is the method you need to create inside your class?
   - @Override

     public void run()
   - public void run
   - @Override

     public void run(String... strings) throws Exception
   - public void run(String... strings) throws Exception

EXERCISE 3.04

Create an application with a model class designed to store cars. Each record should include the fields: year, make and model. Create a data loader class to add 3 records to the table when the application starts.

3.05 DATABASE RELATIONSHIPS - MANY TO MANY

LEARNING OBJECTIVES
- Implementing a Many to Many database relationship in Spring Boot

THE WALKTHROUGH

1. **Create a Spring Boot Application**
   - Name it SpringBoot_305
   - Add the dependencies for the web, jpa, h2 and thymeleaf
   - Hit next until you finish the wizard, and then wait until it's done.

2. **Create a Class**
   - Right click on com.example.demo and click New -> Class
   - Name it Movie.java
   - Edit it to look like this:

   ```
   @Entity
   public class Movie {
       @Id
       @GeneratedValue(strategy = GenerationType.AUTO)
       private long id;
       private String title;
       private long year;
       private String description;

       @ManyToMany
       private Set<Actor> cast;
   }
   ```

3. **Autogenerate getters and setters**
   - Inside your Movie.java file, right-click on the word Movie and select generate -> Getters and Setters
   - Select all the fields listed and click OK

4. **Create a Class**
   - Right click on com.example.demo and click New -> Class
   - Name it Actor.java
   - Edit it to look like this:

   ```
   @Entity
   public class Actor {
       @Id
       @GeneratedValue(strategy = GenerationType.AUTO)
       private long id;
   ```

3.05 DATABASE RELATIONSHIPS - MANY TO MANY

```java
    private String name;
    private String realname;
    @ManyToMany(mappedBy = "cast")
    private Set<Movie> movies;
}
```

5. **Autogenerate getters and setters**
   - Inside your Actor.java file, right-click on the word Actor and select generate -> Getters and Setters
   - Select all the fields listed and click OK

6. **Create a Repository**
   - Right click on com.example.demo and click New -> Class
   - Change the value of the drop-down box to Interface
   - Name it MovieRepository.java
   - Edit it to look like this

   ```java
   public interface MovieRepository extends CrudRepository<Movie,Long>{}
   ```

7. **Create a Repository**
   - Right click on com.example.demo and click New -> Class
   - Change the value of the drop-down box to Interface
   - Name it ActorRepository.java
   - Edit it to look like this:

   ```java
   public interface ActorRepository extends CrudRepository<Actor,Long>{}
   ```

8. **Create a Controller**
   - Right click on com.example.demo and click New -> Class
   - Name it HomeController.java
   - Edit it to look like this:

   ```java
   @Controller
   public class HomeController {

       @Autowired
       ActorRepository actorRepository;

       @Autowired
       MovieRepository movieRepository;
   ```

3.05 DATABASE RELATIONSHIPS - MANY TO MANY

```java
@RequestMapping("/")
public String index(Model model){
    Actor actor = new Actor();
    actor.setName("Sandra Bullock");
    actor.setRealname("Sandra Mae Bullowski");

    Movie movie = new Movie();
    movie.setTitle("Emoji Movie");
    movie.setYear(2017);


    movie.setDescription("About Emojis...");
    Set<Movie> movies = new HashSet<Movie>();
    movies.add(movie);

    actor.setMovies(movies);
    actorRepository.save(actor);

    model.addAttribute("actors", actorRepository.findAll());
    return "index";
    }
}
```

9. **Create a Template**
   - Right click on templates and click New -> Html
   - Name it index.html
   - Edit the empty body tag (<body></body>) to look like this:

```html
<body>
<h1>Movie List</h1>
<div th:each="actor : ${actors}">
    <h2 th:text="${actor.name}"></h2>
    <h6 th:inline="text">AKA [[${actor.realname}]]</h6>
<ul>
    <th:block  th:each="movie : ${actor.movies}">
    <li th:inline="text"><b>[[${movie.title}]]</b> released in [[${movie.year}]].</li>
    </th:block>
</ul>
</div>
</body>
```

10. **Run your application and open a browser, if you type in the URL http://localhost:8080 you should see something like** *Screen 3.05.1.*

3.05 DATABASE RELATIONSHIPS - MANY TO MANY

Movie List

Sandra Bullock

AKA Sandra Mae Bullowski

- **Emoji Movie** released in 2017.

Screen 3.05.1

IMPORTS

AUTOWIRED
`org.springframework.beans.factory.annotation.Autowired`

CRUDREPOSITORY
`org.springframework.data.repository.CrudRepository`

ENTITY
`javax.persistence.Entity`

GENERATEDVALUE
`javax.persistence.GeneratedValue`

GENERATIONTYPE
`javax.persistence.GenerationType`

ID
`javax.persistence.Id`

MANYTOMANY
`javax.persistence.ManyToMany`

MODEL
`org.springframework.stereotype.Component`

SET
`java.util.Set;`

WHAT'S GOING ON?

Our application is tracking actors and movies. Each actor can be in many movies. And each movie can contain many actors. So the relationship between actors and movies in the database is described as Many to Many.

How does a database keep track of which actors go with which movies? We can't add a movie id to the actor table because that would allow only one movie per actor. We can't add an actor id field to the movie table because then there would only be room for one actor in every movie.

The solution? Use annotations to tell Spring Boot what we want.

There's not much we actually have to do because Spring Boot will handle the situation for us using annotations. Annotations are instructions for Spring Boot, letting it know what our intentions are. Spring Boot will read the annotations and create the appropriate tables. The table contains only actor ids and movie ids. So, we could have as many actor/movie combinations as we desire. We should add a limitation that the movie id and actor id combination can only be in the table once but we'll let the database deal with that.

3.05 DATABASE RELATIONSHIPS - MANY TO MANY

Look in the Actor class. Notice the annotation **@ManyToMany(mappedBy = "cast")**? This annotation points back to the Movie class. The Movie class contains a data member for cast of type **Set<Actor>**. This links the two together.

When the database is created it will contain three tables: movie, actor and movie_actor. And all our data will be properly related. And the only thing you did is set some values in annotations. Pretty cool, right?

EXERCISE 3.05

Create an application that shows a many to many relationship between courses and students.

3.06 DATABASE RELATIONSHIPS - ONE TO MANY

LEARNING OBJECTIVES
- Implementing a One to Many database relationship in Spring Boot

THE WALKTHROUGH

1. **Create a Spring Boot Application**
   - Name it SpringBoot_306
   - Add the dependencies for the web, jpa, h2 and thymeleaf
   - Hit next until you finish the wizard, and then wait until it's done.

2. **Create a Class**
   - Right click on com.example.demo and click New -> Class
   - Name it Director.java
   - Edit it to look like this:

   ```
   @Entity
   public class Director {
       @Id
       @GeneratedValue(strategy = GenerationType.AUTO)
       private long id;
       private String name;
       private String genre;

       @OneToMany(mappedBy = "director", cascade = CascadeType.ALL,
                   fetch = FetchType.EAGER)
       public Set<Movie> movies;
   }
   ```

3. **Autogenerate getters and setters**
   - Inside your Director.java file, right-click on the word Director and select generate -> Getters and Setters
   - Select all the fields listed and click OK

3.06 DATABASE RELATIONSHIPS - ONE TO MANY

4. **Create a Class**
   - Right click on com.example.demo and click New -> Class
   - Name it Movie.java
   - Edit it to look like this:

   ```
   @Entity
   public class Movie {
       @Id
       @GeneratedValue(strategy = GenerationType.AUTO)
       private long id;

       private String title;
       private long year;
       private String description;

       @ManyToOne(fetch = FetchType.EAGER)
       @JoinColumn(name = "director_id")
       private Director director;
   }
   ```

5. **Autogenerate getters and setters**
   - Inside your Movie.java file, right-click on the word Movie and select generate -> Getters and Setters
   - Select all the fields listed and click OK

6. **Create a Repository**
   - Right click on com.example.demo and click New -> Class
   - Change the value of the drop-down box to Interface
   - Name it MovieRepository.java
   - Edit it to look like this:

   ```
   public interface MovieRepository extends CrudRepository<Movie,Long>{}
   ```

7. **Create a Repository**
   - Right click on com.example.demo and click New -> Class
   - Change the value of the drop-down box to Interface
   - Name it DirectorRepository.java
   - Edit it to look like this:

   ```
   public interface DirectorRepository extends CrudRepository<Director, Long>{
   }
   ```

3.06 DATABASE RELATIONSHIPS - ONE TO MANY

8. **Create a Controller**
   - Right click on com.example.demo and click New -> Class
   - Name it HomeController.java
   - Edit it to look like this:

```java
@Controller
public class HomeController {

    @Autowired
    DirectorRepository directorRepository;


    @RequestMapping("/")
    public String index(Model model){
        // First let's create a director
        Director director = new Director();

        director.setName("Stephen Bullock");
        director.setGenre("Sci Fi");

        // Now let's create a movie
        Movie movie = new Movie();
        movie.setTitle("Star Movie");
        movie.setYear(2017);
        movie.setDescription("About Stars...");

        // Add the movie to an empty list
        Set<Movie> movies = new HashSet<Movie>();
        movies.add(movie);

        movie = new Movie();
        movie.setTitle("DeathStar Ewoks");
        movie.setYear(2011);
        movie.setDescription("About Ewoks on the DeathStar...");
        movies.add(movie);

        // Add the list of movies to the director's movie list
        director.setMovies(movies);

        // Save the director to the database
        directorRepository.save(director);

        // Grab all the directors from the database and send them to
        // the template
        model.addAttribute("directors", directorRepository.findAll());
        return "index";
    }
}
```

3.06 DATABASE RELATIONSHIPS - ONE TO MANY

9. **Create a Template**
   - Right click on templates and click New -> Html
   - Name it index.html
   - Edit it to look like this:

```html
<body>
<h1>Director List</h1>
<div th:each="director : ${directors}">
    <h2 th:text="${director.name}"></h2>
    <h6 th:inline="text">specializing in [[${director.genre}]]</h6>

    <ul>
        <th:block  th:each="movie : ${director.movies}">
            <li th:inline="text"><b>[[${movie.title}]]</b> released in
                [[${movie.year}]].</li>
        </th:block>
    </ul>
</div>
</body>
```

Screen 3.06.1

10. Run your application and open a browser, if you type in the URL http://localhost:8080 you should see something like *Screen 3.06.1*.

3.06 DATABASE RELATIONSHIPS - ONE TO MANY

IMPORTS

AUTOWIRED
org.springframework.beans.factory.annotation.Autowired

CRUDREPOSITORY
org.springframework.data.repository.CrudRepository

ENTITY
javax.persistence.Entity

GENERATEDVALUE
javax.persistence.GeneratedValue

GENERATIONTYPE
javax.persistence.GenerationType

ID
javax.persistence.Id

MODEL
org.springframework.stereotype.Component

ONETOMANY
javax.persistence.OneToMany

SET
java.util.Set;

WHAT'S GOING ON?

Our application is tracking directors and movies. Each director can direct many movies. And each movie can have only one director. So the relationship between actors and movies in the database is described as One to Many. (The way I've written it you could say it's many to one but nobody refers to it that way so bear with me).

How does a database keep track of which movies go with which directors? We can add a director id to the movie table. This will work because we have decided there would be only one director per movie.

The solution? As before, use annotations to configure our application. They tell Spring Boot how to set up the database. Let Spring Boot work out the underlying details.

In the director class we create an annotation for OneToMany and we attach that (by placing it above) to a set of movies. Now each director comes with their own collection of movies.

Why a set? Why not an array list or hash table? A set is a special object in Java. It allows each element to exist only once. So if you tried to add the same movie eighty-billion times you'd still only have one instance of it in the set. The annoyed set would just keep ignoring you. Another thing about the set... order doesn't matter. A list generally implies order. A set just contains items.

What is mappedBy? It tells the set of movies where to save the director data. In other words, the director class is the keeper of the movie set. So, add a **mappedBy="director"** attribute to your Director class to signal to the persistence provider that the join column should be in the Movie table.

What is cascade? The meaning of **CascadeType.ALL** is that the persistence will propagate (cascade) all EntityManager operations (PERSIST, REMOVE, REFRESH, MERGE, DETACH) to the relating entities.

3.06 DATABASE RELATIONSHIPS - ONE TO MANY

When defining relationships between objects you should identify the class that will serve as the owner of the relationship or keeper of the data. You should specify the @JoinColumn annotation in the class that owns the relationship.

What is fetch? Fetching strategies define how related objects are loaded. One director can have multiple movies. In eager loading, if we load the director data, the related movie objects are loaded immediately. In lazy loading, movie objects won't be loaded until they are accessed for the first time.

QUESTIONS

1. You have created an application that has author and book tables that are linked as a one to many relationship. If you wish the associated books to be automatically loaded whenever an author record is retrieved then the you should use which of the following?
   - `cascade = CascadeType.ALL`
   - `fetch = FetchType.EAGER`
   - `fetch = FetchType.LAZY`
   - `cascase = CascadeType.PERSIST`

2. If two tables named Author and Book are linked as an One to Many relationship, which of the following should be used to tell the Book table that it has a field that indicates the id of the author?
   - a @JoinColumn(name = "author_id") annotation in the Book class
   - a @JoinColumn(name = "book_id") annotation in the Author class
   - a @JoinColumn(name = "author_id") annotation in the Author class
   - fetch=FetchType.LAZY

EXERCISE 3.06

Create an application that stores Album and Song data in a One to Many relationship. Add the ability to add, delete and list all songs and all albums. Additionally, add the ability to see all the songs on an album when a single album is viewed.

3.07 DATABASE RELATIONSHIPS - ONE TO ONE

LEARNING OBJECTIVES

- Implementing a One to One database relationship in Spring Boot

THE WALKTHROUGH

1. **Create a Spring Boot Application**
   - Name it SpringBoot_307
   - Add the dependencies for the web, jpa, h2 and thymeleaf
   - Hit next until you finish the wizard, and then wait until it's done.

2. **Create a Class**
   - Right click on com.example.demo and click New -> Class
   - Name it Employee.java
   - Edit it to look like this:

   ```
   @Entity
   public class Employee {
       @Id
       @GeneratedValue(strategy = GenerationType.AUTO)
       private int id;
       private String name;
       private String ssn;

       @OneToOne(cascade = CascadeType.ALL)
       @JoinColumn(name = "laptop_id")
       private Laptop laptop;
   }
   ```

3. **Autogenerate getters and setters**
   - Inside your Employee.java file, right-click on the word Employee and select generate -> Getters and Setters
   - Select all the fields listed and click OK

3.07 DATABASE RELATIONSHIPS - ONE TO ONE

4. **Create a Class**
   - Right click on com.example.demo and click New -> Class
   - Name it Laptop.java
   - Edit it to look like this:

   ```
   @Entity
   public class Laptop {
       @Id
       @GeneratedValue(strategy = GenerationType.AUTO)
       private int id;
       private String brand;
       private String model;

       @OneToOne(mappedBy = "laptop")
       private Employee employee;
   }
   ```

5. **Autogenerate getters and setters**
   - Inside your Laptop.java file, right-click on the word Laptop and select generate -> Getters and Setters
   - Select all the fields listed and click OK

6. **Create a Repository**
   - Right click on com.example.demo and click New -> Class
   - Name it EmployeeRepository.java
   - Edit it to look like this:

   ```
   public interface EmployeeRepository extends CrudRepository<Employee, Long>{}
   ```

7. **Create a Repository**
   - Right click on com.example.demo and click New -> Class
   - Name it LaptopRepository.java
   - Edit it to look like this:

   ```
   public interface LaptopRepository extends CrudRepository<Laptop, Long>{
   }
   ```

3.07 DATABASE RELATIONSHIPS - ONE TO ONE

8. **Create a Controller**
   - Right click on com.example.demo and click New -> Class
   - Name it HomeController.java
   - Edit it to look like this:

   ```
   @Controller
   public class HomeController {

       @Autowired
       EmployeeRepository employeeRepository;

       @RequestMapping("/")
       public String index(Model model){
           // First let's create an employee
           Employee employee = new Employee();
           employee.setName("Stephen Bullock");
           employee.setSsn("555-12-1234");
           Laptop laptop = new Laptop();

           laptop.setBrand("Dell");
           laptop.setModel("Latitude XL");
           employee.setLaptop(laptop);
           employeeRepository.save(employee);

           model.addAttribute("employees", employeeRepository.findAll());
           return "index";
       }
   }
   ```

9. **Create a Template**
   - Right click on templates and click New -> Html
   - Name it index.html
   - Edit it to look like this:

   ```
   <body>
   <h1>Employee List</h1>
   <div th:each="employee : ${employees}">
       <h2 th:text="${employee.name}"></h2>
       <h6 th:inline="text">identified by [[${employee.ssn}]]</h6>
       <ul>
           <th:block th:object="${employee.laptop}" >
               <li th:inline="text">Has been assigned a
               <b>[[*{brand}]]</b> [[*{model}]].</li>
           </th:block>
       </ul>
   </div>
   </body>
   ```

3.07 DATABASE RELATIONSHIPS - ONE TO ONE

10. Run your application and open a browser, if you type in the URL http://localhost:8080 you should see something like *Screen 3.07.1*.

Employee List

Stephen Bullock

identified by 555-12-1234

- Has been assigned a **Dell** Latitude XL.

Screen 3.07.1

WHAT'S GOING ON?

Our application is tracking employees and laptops. Each employee can be assigned one company laptop. And each laptop can have only one employee. So the relationship between employee and laptop in the database is described as One to One.

How does a database keep track of which laptop goes with which employee? We can add a laptop id to the employee table. This will work because we have decided there would be only one laptop per employee.

The solution? As before, use annotations to configure our application. They tell Spring Boot how to set up the database. Let Spring Boot work out the underlying details.

In the employee class we create an annotation for OneToOne and we attach that (by placing it above) to a laptop. Now each employee has their own laptop.

What is mappedBy? It tells the laptop where to save the data. In other words, the employee class is the keeper of the laptop. So, add a `mappedBy="laptop"` attribute to your employee class to signal to the persistence provider that the join column should be in the employee table.

What is cascade? The meaning of CascadeType.ALL is that the persistence will propagate (cascade) all EntityManager operations (PERSIST, REMOVE, REFRESH, MERGE, DETACH) to the relating entities.

When defining relationships between objects you should identify the class that will serve as the owner of the relationship or keeper of the data. You should specify the @JoinColumn annotation in the class that owns the relationship.

3.07 DATABASE RELATIONSHIPS - ONE TO ONE

QUESTIONS

1. **How would a one to one relationship best be represented?**
   - As two tables where one table has a reference to the other
   - As two tables where both tables have references to each other
   - As two main tables with a intervening link table
   - As two main tables with two intervening link tables

   ```
   Person person = new Person();
   person.setName("Stephen Bullock");
   person.setSsn("555-12-1234");

   Passport passport = new Passport();
   passport.setPassportNumber(786756556);
   passport.setExpirationDate("12-4-2020");

   person.setPassport(passport);
   personRepository.save(person);
   ```

2. **If the above code is in your program, which of the following must be true?**
   - The Person class has a link field to Passport class
   - The Passport class has a link field to the Person class

EXERCISE 3.07

Create an application that stores person and passport data in a one to one relationship.

4.0 SECURITY TOOLS

4.01 Basic Security
4.02 Adding a Custom Login Page
4.03 Using Roles for Page Permissions
4.04 Using Database-based Authentication
4.05 Persisting Current User Information
4.06 Implementing User Registration

4.01 BASIC SECURITY

LEARNING OBJECTIVES
- Setting up basic Spring Boot Security
- Adding manual user accounts

THE WALKTHROUGH

1. **Create a Spring Boot Application**
   - Name it SpringBoot_401
   - Add the dependencies for web and thymeleaf
   - Select the dependency for security
     - **On the left column click on Security and then click the checkbox next to Spring Security**
     - **Click the Next button in the lower right hand corner**
   - Hit next until you finish the wizard, and then wait until it's done.

2. **Create a SecurityConfiguration Class**
   - Right click on com.example.demo and click New -> Class
   - Name it SecurityConfiguration.java
   - Edit it to look like this:

```java
@Configuration
@EnableWebSecurity
public class SecurityConfiguration extends WebSecurityConfigurerAdapter{

    @Bean
    public static BCryptPasswordEncoder passwordEncoder(){
        return new BCryptPasswordEncoder();
    }

    @Override
    protected void configure(HttpSecurity http) throws Exception {
        http
                .authorizeRequests().anyRequest().authenticated()
                .and().formLogin();
    }

    @Override
    protected void configure(AuthenticationManagerBuilder auth)
    throws Exception{
        auth.inMemoryAuthentication().withUser("user")
        .password(passwordEncoder().encode("password")).authorities("USER");
    }
}
```

4.01 BASIC SECURITY

3. **Create a Controller**
   - Right click on com.example.demo and click New -> Class
   - Name it HomeController.java
   - Edit it to look like this:

   ```
   @Controller
   public class HomeController {
       @RequestMapping("/")
       public String index(){
           return "index";
       }
   }
   ```

4. **Create a Template**
   - Right click on templates and click New -> Html
   - Name it index.html
   - Edit the empty body tag (<body></body>) to look like this:

   ```
   <body>
       <h2>It works!</h2>
   </body>
   ```

5. Run your application and open a browser, if you type in the URL http://localhost:8080 you should see something like *Screen 4.01.1*.

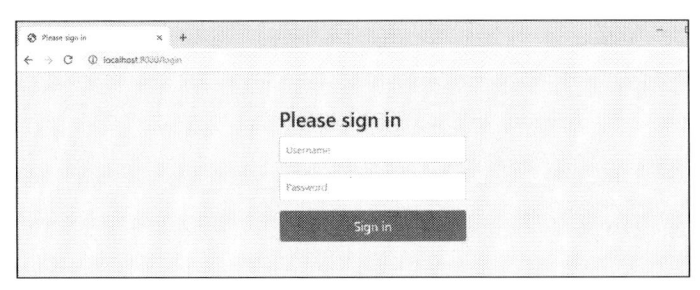

Screen 4.01.1

4.01 BASIC SECURITY

IMPORTS

AUTHENTICATIONMANAGERBUILDER
org.springframework.security.config.annotation.authentication.builders.AuthenticationManagerBuilder

BCRYPTPASSWORDENCODER
org.springframework.security.crypto.bcrypt.BCryptPasswordEncoder

BEAN
org.springframework.context.annotation.Bean

CONFIGURATION
org.springframework.context.annotation.Configuration

CONTROLLER
org.springframework.stereotype.Controller

ENABLEWEBSECURITY
org.springframework.security.config.annotation.web.configuration.EnableWebSecurity

HTTPSECURITY
org.springframework.security.config.annotation.web.builders.HttpSecurity

REQUESTMAPPING
org.springframework.web.bind.annotation.RequestMapping

WEBSECURITYCONFIGURERADAPTER
org.springframework.security.config.annotation.web.configuration.WebSecurityConfigurerAdapter

WHAT'S GOING ON

Congratulations! You're ready to add basic security to your Spring Boot web application. This will help to ensure that people are who they say they are (because they use the appropriate passwords to sign in), and that they can access information within your application because they are authorized to have access to it, since they are assigned authorities.

In this example, you will use Spring Boot's default security options, with a little customisation. You will set your own username and password for accessing the application using in-memory authentication. This means your username and password details will not be stored in a database, but you will be able to use them every time that appication runs.

When users are created (either as in-memory users or in a database), they have at least one, but possibly many authorities assigned to them. These authorities can restrict appication access even further.

The new addition - SecurityConfiguration.java

This is a file that sets up the applicaition to restrict access. By default, if access is not specified, it is denied. You have to specifically permit access to each page, directory or group of pages in your application.

@Configuration and **@EnableWebSecurity** This indicates to the compiler that the file is a configuration file and Spring Security is enabled for the application.

The class you create (SecurityConfiguration) extends the WebSecurityConfigurerAdapter, which has all of the methods needed to include security in your application.

4.01 BASIC SECURITY

.authorizeRequests() This tells your application which requests should be authorized. In this example, you are telling the application that any request that is authenticated should be permitted. Right now, this means that if a user enters a correct user/password combination, he/she will be directed to the default route.

.and() Adds additional authentication rules. Use this to combine rules.

.formLogin() This indicates that the application should show a login form. Spring Boot's default login form will be shown, and this will include messages for incorrect attempts.

configure() This overrides the default configure method, configures users who can access the application. By default, Spring Boot will provide a new random password assigned to the user "user" when it starts up, if you do not include this method.

Once you include this method, you will be able to log in with the users configured here. At this point, the configuration is for a single in-memory user. Multiple users can be configured here.

This is also the method in which you can configure how users are granted access to the application if their details are stored in a database.

@Bean and passwordEncoder() method

This creates an object that can be re-used to encode passwords in your application. The encode method is called to provide an instance of a BCyrptPasswordEncoder, which is a password encoder that uses the BCrypt hashing function.

EXERCISE 4.01

Create an application that uses basic security. Check that you can only see the login page if you haven't logged in and that you can then visit any page once you have logged in.

4.02 ADDING A CUSTOM LOGIN PAGE

LEARNING OBJECTIVES
- Creating a custom login page

THE WALKTHROUGH

1. **Start with the code from the previous lesson**

2. **Edit the SecurityConfiguration Class**
   - Add the following on the end of line that reads .formLogin()

   ```
   .loginPage("/login").permitAll()
   ```

   - So it should look like this:

   ```
   @Override
   protected void configure(HttpSecurity http) throws Exception {
       http
               .authorizeRequests().anyRequest().authenticated()
               .and().formLogin().loginPage("/login").permitAll();
   }
   ```

3. **Edit the Controller**
   - Open the HomeController.java file
   - Add the following right before the last }

   ```
   @RequestMapping("/login")
   public String login(){
       return "login";
   }
   ```

   - So it should look like this:

   ```
   @Controller
   public class HomeController {
       @RequestMapping("/")
       public String index(){
           return "index";
       }
       @RequestMapping("/login")
       public String login(){
           return "login";
       }
   }
   ```

4.02 ADDING A CUSTOM LOGIN PAGE

4. **Create a a new Template**
   - Right click on templates and click New -> Html
   - Name it login.html
   - Edit it to look like this:

```html
<body>
    <h1>Login Page</h1>
    <div th:if="${param.error}">
        Invalid username or password
    </div>
    <div th:if="${param.logout}">
        You have been logged out
    </div>
<form th:action="@{/login}" method="post">
    <div><label>User name: <input type="text" name="username"/>
        </label></div>


    <div><label>Password: <input type="password" name="password"/>
        </label></div>
    <div><input type="submit" value="Sign in"/></div>
</form>
</body>
```

5. Run your application and open a browser, if you type in the URL http://localhost:8080 you should see *Screen 4.02.1*.

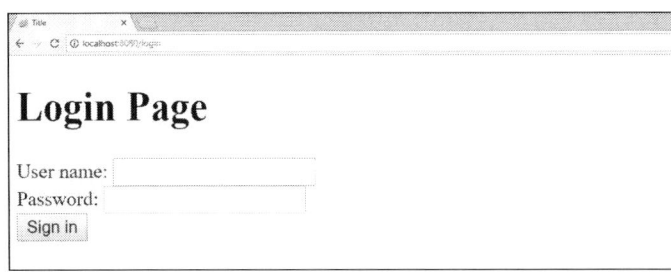

Screen 4.02.1

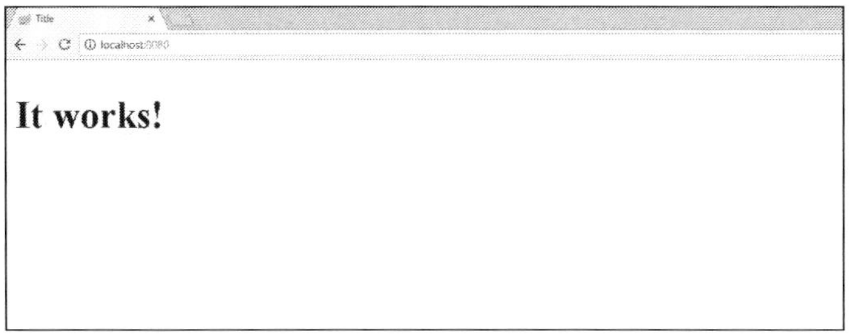

Screen 4.02.2

6. If you successfully login(using the accounts created in the SecurityConfiguration file), you will see *Screen 4.02.2*.

4.02 ADDING A CUSTOM LOGIN PAGE

IMPORTS

AUTHENTICATIONMANAGERBUILDER
org.springframework.security.config.annotation.authentication.builders.AuthenticationManagerBuilder

BCRYPTPASSWORDENCODER
org.springframework.security.crypto.bcrypt.BCryptPasswordEncoder

BEAN
org.springframework.context.annotation.Bean

CONFIGURATION
org.springframework.context.annotation.Configuration

CONTROLLER
org.springframework.stereotype.Controller

ENABLEWEBSECURITY
org.springframework.security.config.annotation.web.configuration.EnableWebSecurity

HTTPSECURITY
org.springframework.security.config.annotation.web.builders.HttpSecurity

REQUESTMAPPING
org.springframework.web.bind.annotation.RequestMapping

WEBSECURITYCONFIGURERADAPTER
org.springframework.security.config.annotation.web.configuration.WebSecurityConfigurerAdapter

WHAT'S GOING ON

You have used Spring Boot's default security page to log in (Lesson 4.01), but if you're building a real world application, you'll want to customise the login form. Once you've got basic security set up, adding a login form is a simple process. First, you have to create the login form. Since this page will receive user input and pass it on to Spring Security, it will need to have fields that Spring Security can use for authentication - specifically, 'username' and 'password'. It will also have to POST the form details to the login route.

Security Configuration Class

The modification you make to this page is as follows: `.formLogin().loginPage("/login").permitAll()` This means that you are expecting a login form, which will display when you visit the route /login, and everyone can see it, even if they are not authenticated.

This is therefore the page that people will see if they have not logged in yet, before they are directed to the page that they can see after logging in.

Login form

This form is displayed when users visit a page that requires authentication. This passes the information on to Spring Security, and if the user name and password are correct, the user is allowed to see the page. If the user enters incorrect details, they will see a message indicating that the login details were incorrect. The code below displays an error message if the login details are incorrect.

4.02 ADDING A CUSTOM LOGIN PAGE

```
<div th:if="${param.error}">
         Invalid username and password.
</div>
```

EXERCISE 4.02

Create an application that uses a custom login form with the title my Login Form.

4.03 USING ROLES FOR PAGE PERMISSIONS

LEARNING OBJECTIVES
- Implementing role-based permissions
- Designating users with specific authorities

THE WALKTHROUGH

1. **Start with the code from the previous lesson**

2. **Edit the SecurityConfiguration Class**
   - Add the following after the line that reads .authorizeRequests()

     ```
     .antMatchers("/").access("hasAnyAuthority('USER','ADMIN')")
     .antMatchers("/admin").access("hasAuthority('ADMIN')")
     ```

   - So the HttpSecurity configure method should look like this when you are done:

     ```
     @Override
     protected void configure(HttpSecurity http) throws Exception
     {
         http.authorizeRequests()
                 .antMatchers("/")
                 .access("hasAnyAuthority('USER','ADMIN')")
                 .antMatchers("/admin")
                 .access("hasAuthority('ADMIN')")
                 .anyRequest().authenticated()
                 .and()
                 .formLogin().loginPage("/login").permitAll()
                 .and()
                 .logout().logoutRequestMatcher(new AntPathRequestMatcher("/logout"))
                 .logoutSuccessUrl("/login").permitAll();
     }
     ```

   - Add the following code after the line that reads auth.inMemoryAuthentication().

     ```
     withUser("dave").password(passwordEncoder().encode("begreat"))
     .authorities("ADMIN").and().
     ```

   - So the AuthenticationManagerBuilder configure method should look like this:

     ```
     @Override
     protected void configure (AuthenticationManagerBuilder auth) throws Exception
     {
         auth.inMemoryAuthentication()
             .withUser("dave").password(passwordEncoder().encode("begreat"))
                 .authorities("ADMIN")
     ```

4.03 USING ROLES FOR PAGE PERMISSIONS

```
        .and().withUser("user").password(passwordEncoder().encode("password"))
            .authorities("USER");
}
```

3. **Edit the Controller**
   - Open the HomeController.java file
   - Add the following right before the last }

   ```
   @RequestMapping("/admin")
   public String admin(){
       return "admin";
   }
   ```

   - So it should look like this:

   ```
   @Controller
   public class HomeController {
       @RequestMapping("/")
       public String index(){
           return "index";
       }

       @RequestMapping("/login")
       public String login(){
           return "login";
       }

       @RequestMapping("/admin")
       public String admin(){
           return "admin";
       }
   }
   ```

4. **Create a Template**
   - Right click on templates and click New -> Html
   - Name it admin.html
   - Edit it to look like this:

   ```
   <body>
       <h2>Admin Page</h2>
   </body>
   ```

4.03 USING ROLES FOR PAGE PERMISSIONS

5. Run your application and open a browser, if you type in the URL http://localhost:8080 Login as user / password you should not be able to navigate to the Admin page. However, if you login as admin / password you should be able to navigate to the Admin Page.

IMPORTS

AUTHENTICATIONMANAGERBUILDER
org.springframework.security.config.annotation.authentication.builders.AuthenticationManagerBuilder

BCRYPTPASSWORDENCODER
org.springframework.security.crypto.bcrypt.BCryptPasswordEncoder

BEAN
org.springframework.context.annotation.Bean

CONFIGURATION
org.springframework.context.annotation.Configuration

CONTROLLER
org.springframework.stereotype.Controller

ENABLEWEBSECURITY
org.springframework.security.config.annotation.web.configuration.EnableWebSecurity

HTTPSECURITY
org.springframework.security.config.annotation.web.builders.HttpSecurity

REQUESTMAPPING
org.springframework.web.bind.annotation.RequestMapping

WEBSECURITYCONFIGURERADAPTER
org.springframework.security.config.annotation.web.configuration.WebSecurityConfigurerAdapter

WHAT'S GOING ON

hasAuthority specifies who has access to the antMatchers request. We specify access to "/admin" only for users with "ADMIN" role.

hasAnyAuthority allows for all roles to access the antMatchers request, in this lesson the request for ("/") can be accessed by both roles, therefore the html page return can be seen by both roles.

The difference between the regular index and the admin page is due to authority of the user and whether they have the roles necessary to view the page.

The order of the rule matters, and the more specific ones go last. Anyone with ADMIN or USER role/authority can access the "/" path, but only those with the ADMIN role/authority can access the "/admin" path.

Besides these two "/" and "/admin" specifications, any request needs to be authenticated.

.access() method specifies who to give access to

.permitAll() method gives unrestricted access to specified page

.hasAuthority() returns true if logged in user has specified authority

4.03 USING ROLES FOR PAGE PERMISSIONS

`.hasAnyAuthority()` returns true if logged in user, or principal, has any of the specified authorities./roles

`.logoutSuccessUrl()` specifies where to redirect the page to after user logs out successfully

We've create a new user called "dave" with the authority of an ADMIN in the configure method.

EXERCISE 4.03

Create an application that 3 pages: a course page, a teacher page and a student page. Also create 3 users: one with ADMIN role, one with USER role and one with both. Finally, set the permissions on your security so that only people with the admin role can see the teacher page and only people with the user role can see the student page.

4.04 USING DATABASE-BASED AUTHENTICATION

LEARNING OBJECTIVES
- Implementing database-based permissions

THE WALKTHROUGH

1. **Start with the code from the previous lesson**

2. **Setup H2**
   - Add the dependencies by opening the pom.xml file and adding the following xml right before the line that reads: </dependencies>

   ```xml
   <dependency>
       <groupId>org.springframework.boot</groupId>
       <artifactId>spring-boot-starter-data-jpa</artifactId>
   </dependency>
   <dependency>
       <groupId>com.h2database</groupId>
       <artifactId>h2</artifactId>
       <scope>runtime</scope>
   </dependency>
   ```

   - Edit the application.properties file to look like this:

   ```
   spring.h2.console.enabled=true
   spring.h2.console.path=/h2-console
   spring.jpa.hibernate.ddl-auto=create
   ```

3. **Import your maven dependencies:**
   - Either click the Import Changes link in the lower right hand corner, or
   - Right-click your project and click Maven -> Re-Import
   - Wait for the background tasks to complete

4. **Create the User Class**
   - Right click on com.example.demo and click New -> Class
   - Name it User.java
   - Edit it to look like this:

   ```java
   @Entity
   @Table(name="User_Data")
   public class User {
   ```

4.04 USING DATABASE-BASED AUTHENTICATION

```java
@Id
@GeneratedValue(strategy = GenerationType.AUTO)
private long id;

@Column(name = "email", nullable = false)
private String email;

@Column(name = "password")
private String password;

@Column(name = "first_name")
private String firstName;

@Column(name = "last_name")
private String lastName;

@Column(name = "enabled")
private boolean enabled;

@Column(name = "username")
private String username;

@ManyToMany(fetch = FetchType.EAGER)
@JoinTable(joinColumns = @JoinColumn(name = "user_id"),
        inverseJoinColumns = @JoinColumn(name = "role_id"))
private Collection<Role> roles;

public User() {
}

public User(String email, String password, String firstName,
   String lastName, boolean enabled, String username) {
     this.setEmail(email);
     this.setPassword(password);
     this.setFirstName(firstName);
     this.setLastName(lastName);
     this.setEnabled(enabled);
     this.setUsername(username);
  }
}
```

NOTE

- Don't add an import for the Role class. You can add it after you have created your Role class in step 6.

4.04 USING DATABASE-BASED AUTHENTICATION

5. **Autogenerate getters and setters**
   - Inside your User.java file, right click on the word User and select Generate -> Getters and Setters
   - Change the setter method for SetPassword to look like this:

   ```java
   public void setPassword(String password) {
       BCryptPasswordEncoder passwordEncoder = new BCryptPasswordEncoder();
       this.password = passwordEncoder.encode(password);
   }
   ```

6. **Create the Role Class**
   - Right click on com.example.demo and click New -> Class
   - Name it Role.java
   - Edit it to look like this:

   ```java
   @Entity
   public class Role {
       @Id
       @GeneratedValue(strategy = GenerationType.AUTO)
       private long id;

       @Column(unique=true)
       private String role;

       @ManyToMany(mappedBy = "roles", fetch = FetchType.LAZY)
       private Collection<User> users;
       public Role() {
       }
       public Role(String role) {
           this.role = role;
       }
   }
   ```

7. **Autogenerate getters and setters**
   - Inside your Role.java file, right click on the word Role and select Generate -> Getters and Setters
   - Click Generate -> Getters and Setters

8. **Create a User Repository**
   - Right click on com.example.demo and click New -> Class
   - Name it UserRepository.java
   - Edit it to look like this:

   ```java
   public interface UserRepository extends CrudRepository<User, Long>{
       User findByUsername(String username);
   }
   ```

4.04 USING DATABASE-BASED AUTHENTICATION

9. **Create a Role Repository**
   - Right click on com.example.demo and click New -> Class
   - Name it RoleRepository.java
   - Edit it to look like this:

```java
public interface RoleRepository extends CrudRepository<Role, Long>{
    Role findByRole(String role);
}
```

10. **Edit the SecurityConfiguration Class**

Edit the class to look like this:

```java
@Configuration
@EnableWebSecurity
public class SecurityConfiguration extends WebSecurityConfigurerAdapter {

    @Bean
    public BCryptPasswordEncoder passwordEncoder() {
        return new BCryptPasswordEncoder();
    }

    @Autowired
    private SSUserDetailsService userDetailsService;

    @Autowired
    private UserRepository userRepository;

    @Override
    public UserDetailsService userDetailsServiceBean() throws Exception {
        return new SSUserDetailsService(userRepository);
    }

    @Override
    protected void configure(HttpSecurity http) throws Exception{
        http
           .authorizeRequests()
           .antMatchers("/", "/h2-console/**").permitAll()
           .antMatchers("/admin").access("hasAuthority('ADMIN')")
           .anyRequest().authenticated()
           .and().formLogin().loginPage("/login").permitAll()
           .and().logout()
           .logoutRequestMatcher( new AntPathRequestMatcher("/logout"))
           .logoutSuccessUrl("/login").permitAll().permitAll()
           .and()
           .httpBasic();
```

4.04 USING DATABASE-BASED AUTHENTICATION

```
            http.csrf().disable();
            http.headers().frameOptions().disable();
        }
        
        @Override
        protected void configure(AuthenticationManagerBuilder auth) throws Exception{
            auth.userDetailsService(userDetailsServiceBean())
                .passwordEncoder(passwordEncoder());
        }
    }
```

11. Create the SSUserDetailsService
- Right click on com.example.demo and click New -> Class
- Name it SSUserDetailsService.java
- Edit it to look like this:

```
@Transactional
@Service
public class SSUserDetailsService implements UserDetailsService{

    private UserRepository userRepository;

    public SSUserDetailsService(UserRepository userRepository){
        this.userRepository=userRepository;
    }

@Override
public UserDetails loadUserByUsername(String username)
        throws UsernameNotFoundException {
    try{
      User user = userRepository.findByUsername(username);
      if (user == null){
        return null;
      }
      return new org.springframework.security.core.userdetails.User(
            user.getUsername(), user.getPassword(), getAuthorities(user)
      );
    } catch (Exception e) {
      throw new UsernameNotFoundException("User not found");
    }
  }

  private Set<GrantedAuthority> getAuthorities(User user) {
    Set<GrantedAuthority> authorities = new HashSet<>();
    for(Role role : user.getRoles()) {
        GrantedAuthority grantedAuthority = new SimpleGrantedAuthority(role.getRole());
```

4.04 USING DATABASE-BASED AUTHENTICATION

```
            authorities.add(grantedAuthority);
        }
        return authorities;
    }
}
```

12. **Edit The Controller**
    - Edit it to look like this:

    ```
    @Controller
    public class HomeController {
        @RequestMapping("/")
        public String index(){
            return "index";
        }

        @RequestMapping("/login")
        public String login(){
            return "login";
        }
        @RequestMapping("/secure")
        public String secure(){
            return "secure";
        }
    }
    ```

13. **Edit The Index Template**
    - Edit it the empty body tag (<body></body>) to look like this:

    ```
    <body>
     <h2>Insecure Page</h2>
     <a href="/secure">Secure Page</a>
    </body>
    ```

14. **Create a Secure Template**
    - Right click on templates and click New -> Html
    - Name it secure.html
    - Edit it the empty body tag (<body></body>) to look like this:

    ```
    <body>
     <h3>Secure Page</h3>
     <a href="/logout">logout</a>
    </body>
    ```

4.04 USING DATABASE-BASED AUTHENTICATION

Screen 4.04.1

Screen 4.04.2

15. **Run your application and open a browser, if you type in the URL http://localhost:8080, you should see *Screen 4.04.01*.**
    - If you click on the secure page link, you should see *Screen 4.04.02*.
    - But you won't be able to login because there are no accounts in the database. To add them, add a dataloader that looks something like this:

```
@Component
public class DataLoader implements CommandLineRunner {
  @Autowired
  UserRepository userRepository;

  @Autowired
  RoleRepository roleRepository;

  @Autowired
  private BcryptPasswordEncoder passwordEncoder;

  @Override
  public void run(String... strings) throws Exception{
    roleRepository.save(new Role("USER"));
    roleRepository.save(new Role("ADMIN"));
    Role adminRole = roleRepository.findByRole("ADMIN");
    Role userRole = roleRepository.findByRole("USER");

    User user = new User("jim@jim.com", "password", "Jim", "Jimmerson", true, "jim");
    user.setRoles(Arrays.asList(userRole));
    userRepository.save(user);

    user = new User("admin@admin.com", "password", "Admin", "User",
        true, "admin");
    user.setRoles(Arrays.asList(adminRole));
    userRepository.save(user);
  }
}
```

   - You should now be able to go to the URL http://localhost:8080/login and login with the credentials jim/password or admin/password.

4.04 USING DATABASE-BASED AUTHENTICATION

WHAT'S GOING ON

In this lesson, we created a User class, Role class and SSUserDetailsService class that work together to have an actual user and role class that allows you to login into the correct page. We hard code this information from the lesson before and allow for Spring to authenticate the information. The last lesson we didn't have a user or role class, but with a DataLoader class, we create user instances that now have email, password, e.t.c stored inside a database that can be authenticated since we don't have a registration form yet. Once we login now, there is an insecure and secure webpage that will say secure.

That was a lot of information.

We created a Java bean for User, which has a many-to-many relationship with roles. Each new user we create will now provide name, password, as well as email and other information. The setter method for the password will look similar to the two-step process we saw in the SecurityConfiguration class.

1. creating an instance of BcryptPasswordEncoder object in passwordEncoder method, and
2. using it to encrypt password in AuthenticationManagerBuilder configure method.

The autowired SSUserDetailsService is used to fetch the user data, which the AuthenticationManagerBuilder uses in tandem with the encrypted passcode to authenticate the user.

REPOSITORIES

- The custom query method findByUserName finds and returns the user by its username for the SSUserDetailsService class.

- And the findByRole query method retrieves the available role and assigns it to the new users as they are created in the dataloader class

4.05 PERSISTING CURRENT USER INFORMATION

LEARNING OBJECTIVES
- Storing User Information when authenticating
- Retrieving information about the current user

THE WALKTHROUGH

1. **Start with the application from the last lesson**
2. **Edit the HomeController to access the data**
   - edit the secure method to look like this:

   ```
   @Autowired
   UserRepository userRepository;

   public String secure(Principal principal, Model model){
   String username = principal.getName();
   model.addAttribute("user", userRepository.findByUsername(username));
   return "secure";
   }
   ```

3. **Edit the secure.html template to access the object**
   - Edit the empty body tag (<body></body>) to look like this:

   ```
   <body>
       <h3>Secure Page</h3>
       <a href="/logout">logout</a>
       <h4>email</h4>
       <p th:text="${user.email}"></p><br/>
       <h4>last name</h4>
       <p th:text="${user.lastName}"></p>
   </body>
   ```

4. **Run your application and open a browser, if you type in the URL http://localhost:8080, you should able to login.** *Screen 4.04.01* Run your application and log in. Navigate to http://localhost:8080/secure.

WHAT'S GOING ON

In this lesson, we learn that we can add custom user details to the security session. The last lesson we were only able to pull out a username and password due to the design of spring security, but now in the session of the current user we are uploading the information into a specific session and providing that information and storing all of it in this current session. The ability to have all the information at hand makes for a more efficient process because there is no additional query that is needed to pull from the entire user database. Simply now

4.05 PERSISTING CURRENT USER INFORMATION

we can use the method **getUser()** to pull the current user information. The new way allows for more flexibility and high scalability for future programs.

A principal is a Java interface that represents an entity, such as a user.

The principal object returns the username, which is then used to fetch the corresponding user object from its repository.

The secure html displays information about the currently authenticated user.

4.06 IMPLEMENTING USER REGISTRATION

LEARNING OBJECTIVES

- Implementing a user registration page for Spring Security

THE WALKTHROUGH

1. **Start with the code from the previous lesson**
2. **Edit the UserRepository**
   - Add these lines to your repository after the line that reads User findByUsername(String username);

   ```
   User findByEmail(String email);
   Long countByEmail(String email);
   Long countByUsername(String username);
   ```

3. **Create a UserService Class(UserService.java)**
   - Right click on com.example.demo and click New -> Class
   - Name it UserService.java
   - Edit it to look like this:

   ```
   @Service
   public class UserService {
     @Autowired
     UserRepository userRepository;

     @Autowired
     RoleRepository roleRepository;

     @Autowired
     private BCryptPasswordEncoder passwordEncoder;

     @Autowired
     public UserService(UserRepository userRepository) {
       this.userRepository = userRepository;
     }

     public User findByEmail(String email) {
       return userRepository.findByEmail(email);
     }
     public Long countByEmail(String email) {
       return userRepository.countByEmail(email);
     }

     public User findByUsername(String username){
       return userRepository.findByUsername(username);
     }
   ```

4.06 IMPLEMENTING USER REGISTRATION

```java
    public void saveUser(User user) {
      user.setRoles(Arrays.asList(roleRepository.findByRole("USER")));
      user.setEnabled(true);
      userRepository.save(user);
    }

    public void saveAdmin(User user) {
      user.setRoles(Arrays.asList(roleRepository.findByRole("ADMIN")));
      user.setEnabled(true);
      userRepository.save(user);
    }
}
```

4. **Edit the HomeController**
   - Add the following after the first {:

```java
@Controller
public class HomeController {

  @Autowired
  private UserService userService;

  @GetMapping("/register")
  public String showRegistrationPage(Model model) {
      model.addAttribute("user", new User());
      return "registration";
  }

  @PostMapping("/register")
  public String processRegistrationPage(@Valid
          @ModelAttribute("user") User user, BindingResult result,
          Model model) {
      model.addAttribute("user", user);
      if (result.hasErrors())
      {
          return "registration";
      }
      else
      {
          userService.saveUser(user);
          model.addAttribute("message", "User Account Created");
      }
      return "index";
  }
}
```

4.06 IMPLEMENTING USER REGISTRATION

5. **Edit the SecurityConfiguration file**
   - Edit the line that looks like

   ```
   .antMatchers("/", "/h2-console/**").permitAll()
   ```

   - to look like this:

   ```
   .antMatchers("/", "/h2-console/**", "/register").permitAll()
   ```

6. **Create a Registration Template**
   - Right click on templates and click New -> Html
   - Name it registration.html
   - Edit the empty body tag (<body></body>) to look like this:

   ```html
   <body>
    <h4>New User Registration</h4>
   <form autocomplete="off"
         action="#"
         th:action="@{/register}"
         th:object="${user}" method="post">

      First Name <mark><strong>
      <span th:if="${#fields.hasErrors('firstName')}"
         th:errors="*{firstName}">First Name Error</span></strong></mark>
      <input type="text" id="firstName" placeholder="First Name"
         th:field="*{firstName}" /><br />

      Last Name <mark><strong>
      <span th:if="${#fields.hasErrors('lastName')}"
         th:errors="*{lastName}">Last Name Error</span></strong></mark>
      <input type="text" id="lastName" placeholder="Last Name"
         th:field="*{lastName}" /><br />

      Email <mark><strong>
      <span th:if="${#fields.hasErrors('email')}"
         th:errors="*{email}">Email Error</span></strong></mark>
      <input type="text" id="email" placeholder="Email"
         th:field="*{email}" />
       <br />

      Username <mark><strong>
      <span th:if="${#fields.hasErrors('username')}"
           th:errors="*{username}">Username Error</span></strong></mark>
      <input type="text" id="username"
           placeholder="Username" th:field="*{username}" /><br />
   ```

4.06 IMPLEMENTING USER REGISTRATION

```html
Password <mark><strong>
<span th:if="${#fields.hasErrors('password')}"
    th:errors="*{password}">Password Error</span></strong></mark>
<input type="text" id="password" placeholder="Password"
    th:field="*{password}" /><br />

<button type="submit" class="btn btn-default">Submit</button>
</form>
</body>
```

7. **Run your application and open a browser**
   - If you type in the URL http://localhost:8080 and you should see your home page:
   - If you click on the secure page link, you should see the login page.
   - But you won't be able to login because there are no accounts in the database. To add them:
     - Navigate to localhost:8080/register
     - Create an account
     - Login using the account you've created
   - Once successfully logged in, you should see the account information that you created in the second HTML page.

WHAT'S GOING ON

In this lesson, we learn how to create a registration form and check it for errors against the java validations. We additionally, create methods inside our repository to validate if the email or username is inside our user repository by counting. The registration form is checked to have valid inputs before being saved. Once a user is created, it allow for the secure page to be opened and accessed which will then display the information you provided.

The UserService class consolidates all services related to the purpose of finding, saving and counting user or role objects. HomeController can look to this class to use both **findByRole** and **findByUsername** query methods without autowiring both repositories for Role and User seperately. We created new route mappings for "/register" with open access to all.

EXERCISE 4.06

Now that you have a complete security template, duplicate this repository and add onto the existing security layer the application layer from the earlier lesson 3.03. Security configuration is complex, so be sure to start in the correct order.

5.0 DESIGN TOOLS

5.01 Using Page Fragments with Thymeleaf

5.02 Adding Twitter Bootstrap using CDNs

5.03 Uploading images with Cloudinary

5.04 Adding Twitter Bootstrap directly

5.05 Custom Error Pages

5.01 USING PAGE FRAGMENTS WITH THYMELEAF

LEARNING OBJECTIVES

- Defining page fragments with Thymeleaf
- Using page fragments with Thymeleaf

THE WALKTHROUGH

1. **Create a Spring Boot Application**
   - Name it SpringBoot_501
   - Add the dependencies for the web and for thymeleaf
   - Hit next until you finish the wizard, and then wait until it's done.

2. **Create a Controller**
   - Right click on com.example.demo and click New -> Class
   - Name it HomeController.java
   - Edit it to look like this:

   ```
   @Controller
   public class HomeController {
       @RequestMapping("/")
       public String index(){
           return "index";
       }

       @RequestMapping("/2")
       public String page2(){
           return "page2";
       }

       @RequestMapping("/3")
       public String page3(){
           return "page3";
       }
   }
   ```

3. **Create a Base Template**
   - Right click on templates and click New -> Html
   - Name it base.html
   - Edit the empty body tag (<body></body>) to look like this:

5.01 USING PAGE FRAGMENTS WITH THYMELEAF

```html
<body>
    <div th:fragment="navlinks">
        <a href="/">index</a> - <a href="/2">Page 2</a> - <a href="/3">Page 3</a>
    </div>
    <div th:fragment="footer">copyright 2017</div>
</body>
```

4. **Create an Index Template**
   - Right click on templates and click New -> Html
   - Name it index.html
   - Edit the empty body tag (`<body></body>`) to look like this:

     ```html
     <body>
         <div th:replace="base :: navlinks"></div>
         <h2>Index Page</h2>
         <div th:replace="base :: footer"></div>
     </body>
     ```

5. **Create a Page2 Template**
   - Right click on templates and click New -> Html
   - Name it page2.html
   - Edit the empty body tag (`<body></body>`) to look like this:

     ```html
     <body>
         <div th:replace="base :: navlinks"></div>
         <h2>Page 2</h2>
         <div th:replace="base :: footer"></div>
     </body>
     ```

6. **Create a Page3 Template**
   - Right click on templates and click New -> Html
   - Name it page3.html
   - Edit the empty body tag (`<body></body>`) to look like this:

     ```html
     <body>
         <div th:replace="base :: navlinks"></div>
         <h2>Page 3</h2>
         <div th:replace="base :: footer"></div>
     </body>
     ```

5.01 USING PAGE FRAGMENTS WITH THYMELEAF

7. Run your application and open a browser, if you type in the URL http://localhost:8080 you should something like *Screen 5.01.1*.

8. And if you click on the Page 2 link, you should see Screen 5.01.2.

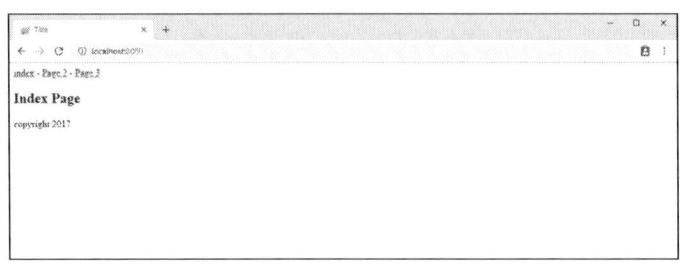

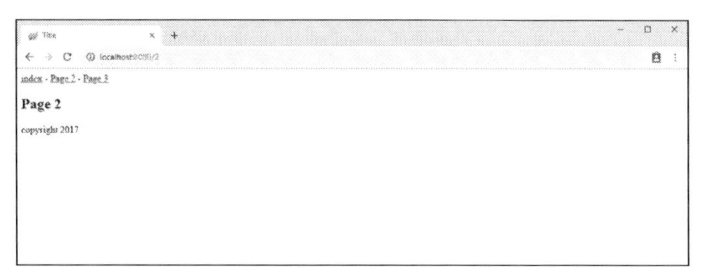

Screen 5.01.1

Screen 5.01.2

IMPORTS

CONTROLLER
org.springframework.stereotype.Controller

REQUESTMAPPING
org.springframework.web.bind.annotation.RequestMapping

WHAT'S GOING ON

Notice that the navigation links and the copyright are the same on every page. If you change the contents of the navlinks div or the footer div in the base.html template and it will change on every page automatically.

On almost any web application, there are pieces of the web page that are duplicated from one page to another. Generally, a site has similar footers, headers and navbars on every page. Building and maintaining a site like this can be challenging when code has to be edited in the exact same way on several different pages.

Page fragments are a way to minimize the confusion. By defining one footer as the footer that is used on every page, it means that all the footers start out the same. It also means that when you change that footer fragment, that the footers on all pages change automatically.

In step 3, we are defining a page fragment in the base.html page by adding th:fragment="navlinks" to the div containing the navbar and th:fragment="footer" to the div containing the footer items. We are now able to refer to these fragments on any other page by including **th:replace** on a page with the **pagename::fragmentname** as the value.

So loading the navlink fragment on a page is done by adding **th:replace="base :: navlinks"** as a tag attribute where we want the fragment inserted.

5.01 USING PAGE FRAGMENTS WITH THYMELEAF

EXERCISE 5.01

Create an application where you have a fragment for the header title and a fragment for the navlinks. The application should have an about page, an index page and a contact us page.

5.02 ADDING TWITTER BOOTSTRAP USING CDNS

LEARNING OBJECTIVES
- Using an html framework with Spring Boot

THE WALKTHROUGH

1. **Create a Spring Boot Application**
   - Name it SpringBoot_502
   - Add the dependencies for the web and thymeleaf
   - Hit next until you finish the wizard, and then wait until it's done.

2. **Create a Controller**
   - Right click on com.example.demo and click New -> Class
   - Name it HomeController.java
   - Edit it to look like this:

   ```
   @Controller
   public class HomeController {
       @RequestMapping("/")
       public String index(){
           return "index";
       }
   }
   ```

3. **Create a Template**
   - Right click on templates and click New -> Html
   - Name it index.html
   - Edit it to look like this:

   ```
   <!DOCTYPE html>
   <html lang="en">
   <head>
       <meta charset="utf-8" />
       <meta http-equiv="X-UA-Compatible" content="IE=edge" />
       <title>Bootstrap 101 Template</title>
   </head>
   <body>
      <div class="container">
        <div class="jumbotron">
           <h1>Hello, world!</h1><p>...</p>
           <p><a class="btn btn-primary btn-lg" href="#" role="button">Learn more</a>
         </p>
         </div>
      </div>
   </body>
   </html>
   ```

5.02 ADDING TWITTER BOOTSTRAP USING CDNS

- Go to http://getbootstrap.com/docs/4.1/getting-started/introduction/ and copy the CSS link and paste that code right above the </head> tag
- Go to http://getbootstrap.com/docs/4.1/getting-started/introduction/ and copy the JS links and paste that code right above the </body> tag
- Note that the CSS link code is not HTML5 compliant. To make it compliant add the closing tag for the element.

4. Run your application and open a browser, if you type in the URL http://localhost:8080 you should see your index page with Twitter Bootstrap.

WHAT'S GOING ON

Congratulations! You have created your first styled HTML page. This is a page that includes the Bootstrap libary, which is a number of CSS and JavaScript files that you can use to style your pages. To find out more about how to style your pages, go to the Twitter Boostsrap website.

The Controller

Here, the default route maps to index.html. The Thymeleaf dependency tells your application that any views from the page will be rendered in HTML, and so the application looks in the templates folder by default, and assumes that the file extension is .html. This is why you do not need to add '.html' to the file name when you display the page.

Your application will display the text of the HTML file in your browser, which will interpret the HTML tags and render (display) them appropriately.

It is particularly important to add the line to make sure that your website is RESPONSIVE, and styles the page according to the dimensions of the device you are using to browse the website. A responsive website means it will shrink and expand to fit the size of whatever screen it is displayed on. This is done automatically and is relatively pain-free for the developer.

The View

The HTML page displays a page that looks a bit better than the others we have seen so far. This is because of Bootstrap.

The CDN (Content Delivery Network) links make sure that the CSS classes are available to the page, so that your application can 'dress up' the HTML file according to the rules laid out. These files are online, and should be easy for your application to access if it is on a sever with access to the internet.

The HTML file interprets these rules using the 'class=' attribute, which indicate what fonts, background styles and images, font size(s), and alignment, among other things, will be used on the page.

5.03 UPLOADING IMAGES WITH CLOUDINARY

LEARNING OBJECTIVES

- Uploading images to Cloudinary
- Retrieving images from Cloudinary
- Transforming Cloudinary images

THE WALKTHROUGH

1. **Create a Spring Boot Application**
   - Name it SpringBoot_503
   - Add the dependencies for web, thymeleaf, jpa and h2
   - Hit next until you finish the wizard, and then wait until it's done.

2. **Sign up for a Cloudinary account (www.cloudinary.com) if you do not already have one**

3. **Manually add Cloudinary dependencies**
   - Open the pom.xml file and add this to the dependencies section

   ```
   <dependency>
       <groupId>com.cloudinary</groupId>
       <artifactId>cloudinary-taglib</artifactId>
       <version>1.2.1</version>
   </dependency>
   <dependency>
       <groupId>com.cloudinary</groupId>
       <artifactId>cloudinary-http44</artifactId>
       <version>1.2.1</version>
   </dependency>
   ```

   - Right-click on pom.xml and go to maven -> reimport

4. **Create a Class**
   - Right-click on com.example.demo and click New -> Class
   - Name it Actor.java
   - Edit it to look like this:

   ```
   @Entity
   public class Actor {
       @Id
       @GeneratedValue(strategy = GenerationType.AUTO)
       private long id;
       private String name;
       private String realname;
       private String headshot;
   }
   ```

5.03 UPLOADING IMAGES WITH CLOUDINARY

5. **Autogenerate getters and setters**
   - Right-click on the word Actor and select generate -> Getters and Setters
   - Select all the fields list and click OK

6. **Create a Repository**
   - Right click on com.example.demo and click New -> Class
   - Name it ActorRepository.java
   - Edit it to look like this:

   ```java
   public interface ActorRepository extends CrudRepository<Actor, Long> {
   }
   ```

7. **Create a Cloudinary Class**
   - Right-click on com.example.demo and click New -> Class
   - Name it CloudinaryConfig.java
   - Edit it to look like this:

   ```java
   @Component
   public class CloudinaryConfig {
       private Cloudinary cloudinary;
       @Autowired
       public CloudinaryConfig(@Value("${cloud.key}") String key,
                               @Value("${cloud.secret}") String secret,
                               @Value("${cloud.name}") String cloud){
           cloudinary = Singleton.getCloudinary();
           cloudinary.config.cloudName=cloud;
           cloudinary.config.apiSecret=secret;
           cloudinary.config.apiKey=key;
       }
       public Map upload(Object file, Map options){
           try{
               return cloudinary.uploader().upload(file, options);
           } catch (IOException e) {
               e.printStackTrace();
               return null;
           }
       }
       public String createUrl(String name, int width,
                               int height, String action){
           return cloudinary.url()
                   .transformation(new Transformation()
                   .width(width).height(height)
                   .border("2px_solid_black").crop(action))
                   .imageTag(name);
       }
   }
   ```

5.03 UPLOADING IMAGES WITH CLOUDINARY

8. **Edit the Configuration**
   - Open the application.properties file
   - Edit it to look like this (keep in mind that you need to replace the placeholders *your cloud name*, *your api secret*, and *your api key* with the values from Cloudinary Dashboard (so the first line would look something like cloud.name=HF*IE<KI738) :

   ```
   cloud.name=your cloud name
   cloud.secret=your api secret
   cloud.key=your api key
   spring.h2.console.path=/h2-console
   spring.h2.console.enabled=true
   ```

9. **Create a Controller**
   - Right-click on com.example.demo and click New -> Class
   - Name it HomeController.java
   - Edit it to look like this:

   ```
   @Controller
   public class HomeController {
       @Autowired
       ActorRepository actorRepository;

       @Autowired
       CloudinaryConfig cloudc;

       @RequestMapping("/")
       public String listActors(Model model){
           model.addAttribute("actors", actorRepository.findAll());
           return "list";
       }

       @GetMapping("/add")
       public String newActor(Model model){
           model.addAttribute("actor", new Actor());
           return "form";
       }
       @PostMapping("/add")
       public String processActor(@ModelAttribute Actor actor,
         @RequestParam("file")MultipartFile file){
           if (file.isEmpty()){
               return "redirect:/add";
           }
           try {
               Map uploadResult =  cloudc.upload(file.getBytes(),
                   ObjectUtils.asMap("resourcetype", "auto"));
               actor.setHeadshot(uploadResult.get("url").toString());
               actorRepository.save(actor);
   ```

5.03 UPLOADING IMAGES WITH CLOUDINARY

```
        } catch (IOException e){
            e.printStackTrace();
            return "redirect:/add";
        }
        return "redirect:/";
    }
}
```

10. **Create a Template for the actor listings**
    - Right click on templates and click New -> Html
    - Name it list.html
    - Edit the empty body tag (<body></body>) to look like this:

    ```
    <body>
    <a href="/add">Add an actor</a>
      <div th:each="actor : ${actors}">
         <div th:if="${actor.headshot} != null">
            <img th:src="${actor.headshot}" /><hr />
         </div>
         <h3 th:text="${actor.name}"></h3><h4 th:text="${actor.realname}"></h4>
      </div>
    </body>
    ```

11. **Create a Template for the actor form**
    - Right click on templates and click New -> Html
    - Name it form.html
    - Edit it to look like this:

    ```
    <body>
      <br /><br />
      <h1>Spring Boot file upload example</h1>
      <form method="POST" action="/add" th:object="${actor}"
             enctype="multipart/form-data">
         Name: <input type="text" th:field="*{name}" />
         Real Name: <input type="text" th:field="*{realname}" />
         <input type="file" name="file" /><br/><br/>
         <input type="submit" value="Submit" />
      </form>
    </body>
    ```

5.03 UPLOADING IMAGES WITH CLOUDINARY

12. Run your application and open a browser, it you type in the URL http://localhost:8080 you should see *Screen 5.03.1*.

13. If you enter the values and upload an image, it will show you a list of all the actors added so far. So, you should see a page that looks like *Screen 5.03.2*.

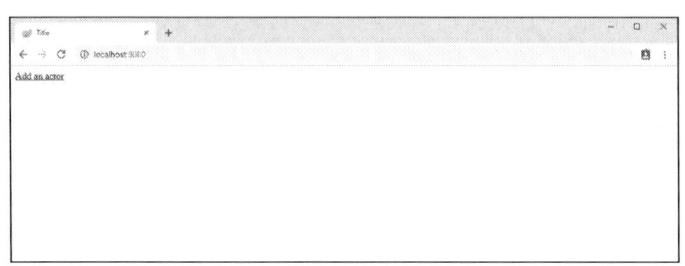

Screen 5.03.1

Screen 5.03.2

IMPORTS

AUTOWIRED
org.springframework.beans.factory.annotation.Autowired

CLOUDINARY
com.cloudinary.Cloudinary

COMPONENT
org.springframework.stereotype.Component

CONTROLLER
org.springframework.stereotype.Controller

ENTITY
javax.persistence.Entity

GENERATEDVALUE
javax.persistence.GeneratedValue

IMPORTS (CONT)

IOEXCEPTION
java.io.IOException

ID
javax.persistence.Id

MAP
java.util.Map

MODEL
org.springframework.ui.Model

MULTIPARTFILE
org.springframework.web.multipart.MultipartFile

OBJECTUTILS
com.cloudinary.utils.ObjectUtils

SINGLETON
com.cloudinary.Singleton

TRANSFORMATION
com.cloudinary.Transformation

VALUE
org.springframework.beans.factory.annotation.Value

WHAT'S GOING ON

Congratulations! If you've made it this far, you're ready to start using your first third party API. Cloudinary is an application that allows you to upload and transform images, so you can allow your users to filter images, re-shape them, add text, and have a lot of fun using the additional options that come for 'free' with this application.

5.03 UPLOADING IMAGES WITH CLOUDINARY

This is a sample of things you can do with Cloudinary (http://www.cloudinary.com/cookbook) Have fun!

All you need to do is upload the image to the Cloudianry server, and apply as many styles as you would like to to transform the image.

You will need to add the Cloudinary dependency so that you can create an instance of the Cloudinary class. This creates a way for your code to access all of the methods it needs to be able to 'talk to' the Cloudinary server.

In this example, we're creating a database of headshots of actors, so we need to have their names, and a link to their headshots, which will be uploaded via our application and saved to the Cloudinary server.

REMEMBER YOUR GETTERS AND SETTERS!!

You will need to create a class that interacts with the Cloudinary server, and makes all of the transformations available to your application. This class (CloudinaryConfig) will use a number of classes that were imported when you added the dependency to the .pom file.

The Cloudinary Configuration Class

`private Cloudinary cloudinary`

This is an object that will be used to apply your image tranfomations, and generate a URL with those transformations so that you can use the image later.

In the class, you will see the following:

`public CloudinaryConfig()`

This is the constructor for the class you have created. It takes the values of the cloudinary settings you entered in your application.properties file, and assigns those to the variables that the Singleton class will use to connect to Cloudinary.

`public Map upload (Object file, Map options)`

This passes the file from the user's computer to Cloudinary, returning an object which contains all of the properties for the transformed image.

`public String createUrl()`

This creates a Cloudinary URL 'preset' trasnformations. In this case, the width, height and border can automatically be applied each time this method is called, and a URL to the transformed image will be returned.

5.03 UPLOADING IMAGES WITH CLOUDINARY

The Model

Actor

This is a simple entity that saves information about the actor.

The View

list.html

This displays actors' names and pictures. The pictures are displayed using the image tag, but using a thymeleaf attribute, th:src, instead of a regular html attribute.

form.html

This form allows a user to upload files.

`<input type="file">`

indicates that a file is expected, and

`enctype="multipart/form-data"`

indicates that additional data is going to be posted with the form (i.e. the picture). This means that the post variables for the form will include the file which is uploaded. The uploaded file can be processed, as you will see in the PostMapping method for the "add" route.

The Controller

`@RequestMapping("/")`

This route lists all of the actors in the database and displays their images using list.html.

`@GetMapping("/add")`

This route creates an empty object to allow users to add new actors. Users can input these details in form.html.

`@PostMapping("/add")`

This is where the magic happens. Once a user clicks 'submit' on form.html, then the details are submitted to the controller. Here, the file (passed as a request parameter, as it is not part of the model) is uploaded to cloudinary.

The resulting image is saved into a Map called uploadResult (to prepare it for Cloudinary).

`ObjectUtils.asMap("resourcetype","auto")` indicates that Cloudinary should automatically try to detect what kind of file has been uploaded.

5.03 UPLOADING IMAGES WITH CLOUDINARY

Once the file has been successfully saved on the Cloudinary server, and a URL is available, it is saved to the actor object (using the setter for headshot), and the actor model is saved to the database, with the name entered by the user and the file uploaded. The user is then returned to the default route and should see the list of actors and their headshots.

5.04 ADDING TWITTER BOOTSTRAP TO SPRING BOOT

LEARNING OBJECTIVES
- Adding static resources to a Spring Boot application
- Referencing static resources in a Spring Boot application

THE WALKTHROUGH

1. **Start with Lesson 4.01 (an application with basic security)**

2. **Get Twitter Bootstrap**
   - Download the file by using this link: https://github.com/twbs/bootstrap/releases/download/v4.1.3/bootstrap-4.1.3-dist.zip
   - Unzip the file
   - Copy the css, fonts and js folders into the static folder inside the resources folder

3. **Edit the Security Configuration**

   - Open SecurityConfiguration.java
   - After this line:

     ```
     .authorizeRequests()
     ```

   - Add this code:

     ```
     .antMatchers("/", "/css/**", "/js/**").permitAll()
     ```

   - So your code should look something like this:

     ```
     @Configuration
     @EnableWebSecurity
     public class SecurityConfiguration extends WebSecurityConfigurerAdapter {

         @Override
         protected void configure(HttpSecurity http) throws Exception {
             http
                     .authorizeRequests()
                     .antMatchers("/css/**", "/js/**").permitAll()
                     .anyRequest().authenticated()
                     .and().formLogin()
                     .and().httpBasic();
         }
     ```

5.04 ADDING TWITTER BOOTSTRAP TO SPRING BOOT

```java
    @Override
    protected void configure(AuthenticationManagerBuilder auth)
        throws Exception {
        auth.inMemoryAuthentication().withUser("user").password("password").
            authorities("USER");
    }
}
```

4. **Create a Bootstrap Fragment Template**
   - Right click on templates and click New -> Html
   - Name it base.html
   - Edit it to look like this:

```html
<!DOCTYPE html>
<html lang="en" xmlns:th="www.thymeleaf.org">
<head th:fragment="headstuff">
    <meta charset="utf-8" />
    <meta http-equiv="X-UA-Compatible" content="IE=edge" />
    <meta name="viewport" content="width=device-width,
        initial-scale=1" />
    <title>Bootstrap 101 Template</title>
    <link href="/css/bootstrap.min.css" rel="stylesheet" />
    <style>
        body { padding-bottom: 70px; }
    </style>
</head>
<body>
<nav class="navbar navbar-default" th:fragment="navbar">
   <div class="container-fluid">
      <div class="navbar-header">
         <button type="button" class="navbar-toggle collapsed" data-toggle="collapse"
                 data-target="#bs-example-navbar-collapse-1" aria-expanded="false">
            <span class="sr-only">Toggle navigation</span>
            <span class="icon-bar"></span>
            <span class="icon-bar"></span>
            <span class="icon-bar"></span>
         </button>
         <a class="navbar-brand" href="#">LearningByCoding</a>
      </div>

         <div class="collapse navbar-collapse"
              id="bs-example-navbar-collapse-1">
            <ul class="nav navbar-nav">
               <li><a href="/">Home </a></li>
               <li><a href="/secure">Secure </a></li>
            </ul>
            <ul class="nav navbar-nav navbar-right">
```

5.04 ADDING TWITTER BOOTSTRAP TO SPRING BOOT

```html
            <li><a href="/login">Login</a></li>
        </ul>
     </div><!-- /.navbar-collapse -->
   </div><!-- /.container-fluid -->
</nav>

<h1>Hello, world!</h1>

<nav class="navbar navbar-default navbar-fixed-bottom"
     th:fragment="footer">
    <div class="container">
        <ul class="nav navbar-nav">
            <li><a href="/">Home </a></li>
            <li><a href="/secure">Secure </a></li>
            <li><a href="#">(c) 2017 - Learning By Coding</a></li>
        </ul>
    </div>
</nav>

<th:block th:fragment="jslinks">
    <script src=
        "https://ajax.googleapis.com/ajax/libs/jquery/1.12.4/jquery.js">
    </script>
    <script src="/js/bootstrap.js"></script>
</th:block>
</body>
</html>
```

5. **Edit the index Template**
   - Edit it to look like this:

   ```html
   <!DOCTYPE html>
   <html lang="en" xmlns:th="www.thymeleaf.org">
       <head th:replace="base :: headstuff"></head>
       <body>
           <nav th:replace="base :: navbar"></nav>
           <div class="container">
               <div class="jumbotron">
                   <h1>Hello, world!</h1>
                   <p>...</p>
                   <p><a class="btn btn-primary btn-lg"
                         href="/secure" role="button">Go to Secure</a>
                   </p>
               </div>
           </div>
           <nav th:replace="base :: footer"></nav>
           <th:block th:replace="base :: jslinks"></th:block>
       </body>
   </html>
   ```

5.04 ADDING TWITTER BOOTSTRAP TO SPRING BOOT

6. **Create a Error Template**
   - Right click on templates and click New -> Html
   - Name it error.html
   - Edit it to look like this:

   ```
   <!DOCTYPE html>
   <html lang="en" xmlns:th="www.thymeleaf.org">
   <head th:replace="base :: headstuff"></head>
   <body>
   <nav th:replace="base :: navbar"></nav>
   <div class="container"><h1>ERROR</h1><br/>
   </div>
   <nav th:replace="base :: footer"></nav>
   <th:block th:replace="base :: jslinks"></th:block>
   </body>
   </html>
   ```

7. **Edit the Controller**
   - Right click on com.example.demo and click New -> Class
   - Name it HomeController.java
   - Edit it to look like this:

   ```
   @Controller
   public class HomeController {
       @RequestMapping("/")
       public String index(){
           return "index";
       }
   }
   ```

8. Run your application and open a browser, if you type in the URL http://localhost:8080 you should see your home page styled with TwitterBootstrap.
9. Navigate http://localhost:8080/ and you should be redirected to the login page.
10. Once you login with user/password, you should see the jumbotron.

WHAT'S GOING ON

We have shown before (in lesson 5.02) how to add the bootstrap CDN to an insecure website, but Spring security adds another level of complexity. The inclusion of **"/css/**","/js/**").permitAll()** allows for all the files in these folders to be accessed without authentication. You have a css folder and js folder in your static folder and the ** allows for all the files in your css folder and js folder to be permitted. **permitAll()** allows for all these antMatchers requests to be viewed and used without the user logging in.

5.05 CUSTOM ERROR PAGES

LEARNING OBJECTIVES
- Implementing custom error pages

THE WALKTHROUGH

1. **Create a Spring Boot Application**
   - Name it SpringBoot_505
   - Add the dependencies for the web and for thymeleaf
   - Hit next until you finish the wizard, and then wait until it's done.

2. **Create a Controller**
   - Right click on com.example.demo and click New -> Class
   - Name it HomeController.java
   - Edit it to look like this:

   ```
   @Controller
   public class HomeController {
       @RequestMapping("/")
       public String index(){
           return "index";
       }
   }
   ```

3. **Create an Base Template**
   - Right click on templates and click New -> Html
   - Name it base.html
   - Edit it to look like this:

   ```
   <body>
       <div th:fragment="navlinks">
           <a href="/">index</a>
       </div>
       <div th:fragment="footer">copyright 2017</div>
   </body>
   ```

4. **Create an Index Template**
   - Right click on templates and click New -> Html
   - Name it index.html
   - Edit it to look like this:

5.05 CUSTOM ERROR PAGES

```html
<body>
    <div th:replace="base :: navlinks"></div>
    <h2>Index Page</h2>
    <div th:replace="base :: footer"></div>
</body>
```

5. **Create an Error Template**
   - Right click on templates and click New -> Html
   - Name it error.html
   - Edit it to look like this:

```html
<body>
    <div th:replace="base :: navlinks"></div>
    <h2>Error. Page not found</h2>
    <div th:replace="base :: footer"></div>
</body>
```

6. Run your application and open a browser, and type in the URL http://localhost:8080.

7. And if you type in the URL http://localhost:8080/3 you will get an error, since there is not route for that page. By having a template called error, that uses your design and page fragments, you can have error pages that look like the rest of your application.

WHAT'S GOING ON

Spring boot understands that there is a set error page and when you include that into your templates folder it will then read it as the error page without a homecontroller to point towards it. We thus set the error page up to look like your other pages through the page fragments lesson. The added features allows for a complete website to have all the functionality like a regular website. The error page will now display whenever there is no explicit mapping from your homecontroller.

6.0 DEPLOYMENT TOOLS

6.01 Deploying to Heroku

6.02 Deploying to AWS

6.01 DEPLOYING TO HEROKU

LEARNING OBJECTIVES
- Installing the Heroku CLI
- Using the Heroku CLI
- Deploying your application to Heroku

THE WALKTHROUGH

1. Start with any application you created from any previous lesson

2. Create a Heroku Account if you don't already have one, go to Heroku.com and create an account

3. Download the Heroku CLI
   - Find the right download for your platform and install it:
   - https://devcenter.heroku.com/articles/heroku-cli

4. Log in to the Heroku CLI
   - Open the Terminal

   ```
   heroku login
   
   Enter your Heroku credentials.
   Email: java@example.com
   Password:
   ```

5. Provision a new Heroku App:
   - Navigate to the directory your application is in
   - Run the following:

   ```
   heroku create
   
   Creating nameless in organization heroku... done, stack is cedar-14
   http://nameless.herokuapp.com/ | git@heroku.com:nameless-8055.git
   ```

6. Deploy your code
   - Run the following:

   ```
   git push heroku master
   ```

7. Open your application
   - Run the following:

   ```
   heroku open
   ```

6.01 DEPLOYING TO HEROKU

WHAT'S GOING ON

Now that you've created an entire application, you probably want to share it with people. Heroku is a free app hosting service that lets you put your application in the cloud. You can create up to 5 free applications on Heroku.

If you already have a GitHub repository for your application, deploying to Heroku is easy. All you need to do (once you have an account) is log in to the terminal and create an application.

6.02 DEPLOYING TO AWS

LEARNING OBJECTIVES

- Compile an executable .jar file
- Create a java application server with Elastic Beanstalk
- Upload your code to AWS
- Configure the server to run your application

THE WALKTHROUGH

1. **Start with any application with an H2 database from any previous lesson. Make sure the server port is set to 5000.**
   - Open your application.properties file
   - If you don't already have it, add the following line:

   ```
   server.port=5000
   ```

2. **Compile your application into a .jar file:**
   - Open up the main project folder in the terminal
   - Type the following:

   ```
   mvnw package
   ```

Your executable .jar file will be created in the target folder.
   - Change the directory to the Target folder and copy the file that ends in SNAPSHOT.jar to the desktop

3. **Create an AWS Account** If you don't already have one, go to aws.amazon.com and create an account

4. **Create an Application**
   - Open the Elastic Beanstalk console with this preconfigured link: https://console.aws.amazon.com/elasticbeanstalk/home#/gettingStarted?applicationName=first-app
   - Fill out the form with the following information:
     ```
     Application name: first-app
     Platform: Java
     Application code: Upload your code
     ```
   - Upload the file you copied to the desktop
   - After the upload completes, click on the Create Application button.
   - Once everything is set up, AWS will redirect you to the Elastic Beanstalk Dashboard. Above the menu you'll find the URL to access the application. Save the URL, you will need it after Step 6.

6.02 DEPLOYING TO AWS

5. **Configure your Application**
   - On the Application Dashboard, click Configuration
   - Click the Modify button next to Software
   - Scroll down to Environment Properties and add the following values:

   SERVER_PORT : 5000

   - Click on the Apply button and wait for AWS to apply the changes. When the update completed successfully message appears, open the URL for your application.

WHAT'S GOING ON

Now that you've created an entire application, you probably want to share it with people. Amazon Web Services is an app hosting service that lets you put your application in the cloud. You can create a free application on AWS as long as it doesn't require too many resources.